ACTIVITIES FOR TEACHING EMOTIONAL,
SOCIAL AND ORGANISATIONAL SKILLS

SET FOR
SUCCESS

FOREWORD BY DAMIAN SANTOMAURO

JOSIE SANTOMAURO AND MARGARET ANNE CARTER

ILLUSTRATED BY CARLA MARINO

Jessica Kingsley *Publishers*
London and Philadelphia

First published in 2011
by Jessica Kingsley Publishers
116 Pentonville Road
London N1 9JB, UK

and

400 Market Street, Suite 400
Philadelphia, PA 19106, USA

www.jkp.com

Library of Congress Cataloging in Publication Data
Santomauro, J. (Josie)
  Set for success : activities for teaching emotional, social and organisational skills / Josie Santomauro and Margaret Carter ; foreword by Damian Santomauro ; illustrated by Carla Marino.
      p. cm.
  Includes bibliographical references.
  ISBN 978-1-84905-058-6 (alk. paper)
  1. Success in children. 2. Social skills in children. 3. Emotional intelligence. 4. Organizational effectiveness. I. Carter, Margaret-Anne. II. Title.
  BF723.S77S36 2011
  372.82--dc22
                            2010036872

British Library Cataloguing in Publication Data
A CIP catalogue record for this book is available from the British Library

ISBN 978 1 84905 058 6

Printed and bound in Great Britain by
MPG Books Group

Contents

Foreword

In primary school I required many visual aids to assist me in my understanding of challenges, and to this day I thrive on timetables and lists. I was faced with many difficulties, such as how to get ready for school, planning for a project, catching the bus and so on. To help me with these challenges, my mother, Josie Santomauro, created many strategies for herself, me and my teachers to use, which really helped through those years. She took advantage of my need for routine in her strategies and that is what made them work for me. It helped me become who I am today – from being told at a young age that I would be unsuccessful in life, to studying at university, holding down a job and having a steady partner.

Because the strategies were very successful with me, my mother turned them into a resource for others. Now, ten years later, that resource is being published internationally. It feels good to know that the challenges I went through inspired a resource that will now help others all around the world.

Damian Santomauro, diagnosed with Asperger Syndrome at age five. Now 21, he is at college, undertaking a PhD in Clinical Psychology researching Autism Spectrum Disorders.

Overview

The *Collins English Dictionary* (2006) defines success as: the achievement of something attempted; a successful person or thing; a triumph; a favourable outcome; being victorious; the consequence, issue, or result, of an endeavour or undertaking; the favourable or prosperous termination of anything attempted; the attainment of a proposed object. Success is a cornerstone of self-belief (Bandura 1997).

In our highly competitive world children tend to see success in terms of being the best, winning, beating others. This is a narrow view of success where only a few children can 'win' (Covington 1992). If children focus solely on this limited definition they run the risk of cutting themselves off from opportunities to succeed.

There are broader views of success that increase children's opportunities for success – and which can operate effectively within the world we live in. Such views include growth and development, improvement, progress, mastering new skills, understanding new things, learning new things, motivation and engagement and reaching personal bests (Nicholls 1989; Martin 2003, 2005).

In this book we advocate aiming for excellence in personal terms, not relative terms. We provide exciting learning activities focusing on building a child's capacity for success. When success is cast in personal terms it becomes achievable and children become motivated to strive to reach it. In fact, when children think there is no chance of success, they are less likely to bother trying, let alone persisting. The same is true for us as adults! Success breeds success, failure promotes failure. When success happens, children are more likely to apply themselves and in turn achieve successful outcomes.

Children who are successful understand the relevance of breaking down large tasks into manageable bite-size parts because smaller chunks are easier to complete than one whole task. They know the importance of planning how long tasks will take and when they will do them. They set goals and are committed to doing what is necessary to achieve them. They see the completion of each chunk of the task as a success. In the process they are developing their competencies and building their capacity for success.

A positive mental attitude is the key ingredient to building a capacity for success. It is a mindset that is optimistic and realistic. Children with success mindsets strive hard for what they want to achieve. They are diligent, resilient in thinking and actions, confident in their abilities, organised in their pursuits, flexible in their thinking, calm in their disposition, determined in their outlook. They plan for success. They are not procrastinators, nor are they flippant in their behaviour. They view the world through 'can do' lenses, rather than 'can't do' or 'can't be' lenses. They have an 'I can do it' attitude and persist when the going gets tough. They gauge their success in terms of personal best achievements rather than in relative terms. There are times through their daily endeavours when they are disappointed and feel discouraged when more effort may be required. This is called being human! What is different about children who are successful in life is that they actively set themselves up for success. They do not allow their disappointments to take over and define them.

It is our conviction that a baseline condition for setting children up for success in life is their capacity to build the success paradigm for themselves. In this book we offer a direct pathway for this to happen. Children will be involved in different learning activities centred round developing their capabilities. They will create their success capacity with the completion of each learning activity.

Our capacity-building approach to success is unique. Adults journey side by side with the children, scaffolding and supporting them to reach a higher level in their learning, ensuring connections are happening with each child in meaningful and respectful ways. Our activities focus on individual, small and large group settings and cater for the spectrum of intelligences. We promote learning both in the home and at school – the more that children generalise their learning across and between contexts, the more potential there is for capacity building. The activities concentrate on building the capabilities that are essential for setting children up for success: getting organised, being persistent, becoming confident, sociability, regulating emotions, attaining independence, communicating effectively, relaxing and energising, and rights and responsibilities.

Social success

Social success is about children learning and mastering new skills to participate effectively in the social world. Children need guidance and social coaching as they learn appropriate ways of behaving and adapting to their environment. This must be direct and specific and given in a manner that appeals to children's learning styles. Getting the children to practise using certain behaviour in real-life contexts and having wide-ranging opportunities to apply their social learning is essential, as is providing children with feedback about the appropriate way to behave. Assessing children's social mastery will inform when help in understanding and learning appropriate behaviour is required.

Children do not start out knowing how to behave in the social world, nor do they know the names of emotions any more than they do the names of animals or toys. This has to be taught so they are able to develop their social emotional capabilities. Children's current knowledge and skills are the beginning point for continuing their learning.

Social mistakes are a natural and necessary part of children's learning; when children make social mistakes this provides opportunities for many lessons on how to do things differently. If adults let these mistakes go unnoticed or do not deal with them directly, they deprive children of valuable learning. Our goal, as adults, is to help children develop self-discipline, the ability to control their own behaviour and to act responsibly, showing respect for oneself and others.

Research including the Australian Scholarships Group's (ASG) *Student Social and Emotional Health Report* (2007) and researchers including Bernard (2004), Martin (2003), Caprara *et al.* (2000) and Damon (1999) identify several similar capabilities as the foundation blocks of social and emotional well-being: organisation, persistence, confidence, sociability, emotion regulation, independence, effective communication, relaxation, rights and responsibilities and thinking positively.

All children have capabilities that can be identified and promoted. Their social emotional wellness is in different respects like that of all others, some others, and no other. Children develop proficiency in each capability at different rates (Anderson 1982; Bellini 2006) and in diverse ways (Gardner 1983, 1993). Some will be novices in terms of development, others intermediate – developing their capabilities – and other children will be established – reaching mastery (i.e. executing skills across contexts independently and in an appropriate manner). Some children may have reached mastery in some capabilities (e.g. positive thinking and relaxing), be novices in others (e.g. sociability and organisation), and/or still be developing their capabilities – intermediate level – in others (e.g. persistence and assertive communication). The stages of learning are summarised in the following table.

Stages of learning	Characteristics of learner
NOVICE	Exerts a great deal of cognitive effort to complete task
	Vulnerable to distraction
	Requires assistance to complete task
	Makes frequent errors
	Completes tasks slowly
INTERMEDIATE	Becomes more independent but still requires a great deal of cognitive effort to complete
	May hesitate between steps of the task, as in attempting to recall the procedure
	Performs task inconsistently
	Makes fewer errors than novice learners; fluency is increased
	Requires instant feedback on task performance
MASTERY	Completes tasks independently with little cognitive effort
	Is able to complete multiple tasks at the same time
	Does not hesitate between tasks or steps of a task
	Increased fluency
	Effortless performance
	Able to complete tasks across various settings and people
	Adapts performances to environmental demands

Sources: Bellini (2006); Anderson (1982)

Children learn more when they are actively involved in a learning task and have many opportunities to practise their new skills and knowledge. They talk about what they are learning, write about it, relate it to past experiences and apply it to their daily lives. They make what they learn part of themselves.

Teaching process

- Children need first to know the capability involved.
- Children need to understand that the capability applies to a particular situation.
- Children need to learn to generalise the capability across different contexts.

Gardner's Eight Intelligence Framework

Word smart	Number smart	Vision smart	Music smart	People smart	Self smart	Body smart	Nature smart
Using language	Solving maths	Creating	Sensitivity to	Interacting	Self-awareness	Playing sport	Making
Reading	problems	artwork	pitch	socially	Self-	Miming	distinctions
Writing	Predicting	Drawing	Timing and	Cooperating	understanding	Acting	in the natural
Speaking	Calculating	Painting	rhythm	Empathy	Goal setting	Making things	world
Creating	Using logic	Creating	Memorising	Leadership	Reflecting		Capacity to
poetry	Experimenting	mental	songs and		Analysing own		recognise flora
Expressing	Analysing	pictures	tunes		learning		and fauna
ideas in words	Categorising	Designs	Creating				Identifying with
		Graphing	sound				nature
		Diagrams	effects				

Skills and activities

Puppets	Problem solving	Bulletin	Clapping	Debates	I like	Draw self	Nature walk
Plays	Mindmapping	boards	Jingles	Interviews	About me	Compare and	Build a garden
Role-playing	Puzzles	Sequential	Raps	Plays	I am	contrast	Discovery table
Reports	Sorting	steps	Chants	Buddies	Feelings	Letter people	Classroom pet
		Maps		Play a game		Relaxation	Managing
		Acronyms		Tell a joke			ecosystems

Source: Adapted from Gardner (1993)

- Children need to shift their attention from one capability to another or a variation of it.

- Children need to be able to think of alternatives to their behaviour choices when carrying out their capability. This involves social problem solving.

Children can learn much from their social mistakes, including what to do differently next time.

- Emphasise what the children can do next time: 'Mistakes happen. How can you hold the cup so you don't spill the milk next time?' (confidence, organisation, persistence capabilities)

- Separate the deed from the doer: 'I love you – I do not like what you are doing right now.' (emotion resilience, thinking positive, relaxation capabilities)

- Give children another chance: 'Let's have another go at working on the collage…' (organisation, thinking positive, rights and responsibilities capabilities)

- Ask questions: 'What happened when…? What did you learn from that? What else can you do?' (effective communication, independence, thinking positive capabilities)

- Model for the children what to do: 'Watch how I put the blocks away. Each block goes in a special place. See? That way all the blocks get packed away.' (sociability, persistence, rights and responsibilities, organisation capabilities)

According to Skiffington and Zeus (2003), the transfer of knowledge, skills and abilities is more likely to occur under the following conditions:

- *Association:* when the individual can associate the new information with something they already know.

- *Similarity:* when the information is similar to material the individual already knows and fits into a logical framework.

- *Degree of original learning:* if the amount of original learning and knowledge is high, it is more likely that the new learning will transfer.

- *Critical attribute element:* when the information contains elements that are critical or beneficial to the individual, learning is more likely to transfer.

- *Organisational culture:* new behaviour is more successfully learned if the organisational culture supports it.

- *Opportunity:* there must be opportunities to perform the new learning.

- *Minimal delay:* there is minimal delay between acquisition and actual use of the new behaviour.

- *Support:* new learning is more successful if individuals receive support.

Interacting

When interacting with children adults need to remember that the ultimate goal of social coaching is achieving learning that endures. Adults can achieve this by adhering to the following guidelines:

- Be attentive and focused on the child.

- Be on the children's level, both physically and mentally

- Use a calm voice and simple language.

- Acknowledge children's efforts and accomplishments.

- Allow children to experience a range of emotions, teaching them healthy ways of expressing these emotions.

- Use questions in ways that provoke the children into thinking for themselves.

- Match the children's competency learning opportunities with their developmental level.

- Cater for all learning styles.

Structure from Chapter 2 and onwards

Each capability is the focus of a separate chapter. Practical learning activities associated with the capability are supplied. Each activity has detailed requirements, explaining how the activity is to be carried out and what equipment or resources are needed. Suggested possible extension activities are also provided. Each chapter follows the same layout:

- Importance of the capability

- List of activities

- Activity objectives

- Worksheet requirements

- Main activity

- Extension activities

You should assist and supervise the children as they work through each exercise in the book.

2 Getting Organised – Science Themed

I'm preparing

Importance of the capability

Getting organised and being organised is about setting goals to do your best, planning your time to achieve your goals and working towards achieving them. When children have learned to be organised they deliberately arrange tasks to be completed in a systematic way. Children set realistic goals, formulate plans, have the necessary resources, seek help if and when necessary and remain committed to seeing goals through to fruition. They stop procrastinating, monitor their efforts and keep track of deadlines.

List of activities

2.1 Organised Observation   –   Planning an activity

2.2 Cues Card   –   Packing for school

2.3 Descriptive Display   –   Weekly timetable

2.4 Systems Schedule   –   Subject daily timetable

2.5 Identification Icons   –   Task buster visual reminders

2.6 Methodical Mapping   –   Homework planner

2.1 Organised Observation – teacher notes

ACTIVITY OBJECTIVES

I'm preparing

- Children understand what needs to be done – what tasks are required for the experiment to be completed successfully.

- Children work out the correct sequence to follow to achieve their desired goal/complete an experiment.

- Children prepare a plan for a task before beginning it.

- Children learn how to follow a plan to complete an experiment.

- Children remember and understand the importance of following the correct sequence.

- Children learn the importance of preparation and organisation.

WORKSHEET REQUIREMENTS

You will need:

- Glass/tumbler
- Water
- Ice cubes
- String
- Salt

MAIN ACTIVITY

This activity helps children learn the importance of following a sequence in a timely manner to achieve a desired outcome/goal. Children calculate the steps and follow them in an orderly manner to achieve the outcome – in this case, a successful experiment. Adults should support children as they learn to manage their time, as they work out what is the first step, second step, third step, etc. in a sequence. The correct sequence is as follows:

1. Fill the glass with water.

2. Place an ice cube in the glass.

3. Dangle the end of the string onto the ice cube.

4. Keep the string still, sprinkle salt onto the ice cube – leave for a few minutes.

5. Lift the string and watch as the ice cube is lifted out of the glass of water.

EXTENSION ACTIVITIES

- Children put their daily routines into a sequence, starting with getting up at the beginning of the day and concluding with going to bed at the end of the day.

- Children can use pictures or symbols in the sequence rather than words.

- Helper leaves steps out of the sequence and asks the children to work out what the missing steps are.

- Helper mixes the sequence up and lets the children put it in the right order.

2.1 Organised Observation

This activity is to show you that planning can help you to be organised. Everything you do needs a plan. Some plans are small, some are big, and they are always step by step and in a particular sequence/order.

I'm preparing

- Help the scientist plan his experiment.
- Look at the plan that is jumbled up and put it into the correct number sequence so that the scientist can successfully complete his experiment.

Fishing for Ice

The scientist is trying to fish an ice cube out of the water with some string without getting his hands wet. Materials your scientist will need: glass/tumbler, water, ice cubes, string and salt.

Steps:

☐ Dangle the end of the string onto the ice cube.

☐ Lift the string and watch as the ice cube is lifted out of the glass of water.

☐ Place an ice cube in the glass.

☐ Keep the string still, sprinkle salt onto the ice cube – leave for a few minutes.

☐ Fill the glass with water.

2.2 Cues Card – teacher notes

ACTIVITY OBJECTIVES

- Children learn to organise their belongings and daily routines.

- Children gain independence as they learn how to organise their own things.

- Children develop their organisation of thinking and timing.

- Children's stress levels are decreased around getting ready for school.

- Routines to foster children's sense of control are introduced.

WORKSHEET REQUIREMENTS

You will need:

- A4 (or larger if required) coloured card (colour preferably chosen by the children)

- Scissors

- Hole puncher

- Pictures/graphics

- Velcro dots

- Laminating device

- Non-permanent marker

- A piece of string/chain

I'm packing my bag

MAIN ACTIVITY

This activity helps children be organised in packing their school bag. Photocopy the worksheet onto coloured card for the children. They familiarise themselves with the weekly cues card to see which things need to be packed in their school bag on which day. Children draw the items or use prepared pictures. Children review the list every evening and ensure all things needed for the next day are packed in their school bag.

EXTENSION ACTIVITIES

- This can be adapted for recreational activities, such as playing football or ballet for example – children should name which equipment/material is needed for specific activities.

- Children choose a sequence for an activity, such as homework time, and create a sequence chart/plan with pictures or symbols.

2.2 Cues Card

This activity will help you pack your school bag by yourself.

Follow the instructions below to create a checklist card that stays with your school bag so you can check it each day.

- Cut out the schedule for the week below.

- Ask your helper to laminate the schedule.

- Punch a hole into a corner of the schedule.

- With a non-permanent marker, write what needs to be packed under the specific days, e.g. Monday is music day, Tuesday is library day, etc., or cut out pictures/graphics and attach them to your schedule with Velcro dots.

- Attach it to your school bag by string or a chain – it can be hanging outside or inside.

Note: The schedule can be changed each week if necessary.

Monday
Tuesday
Wednesday
Thursday
Friday

2.3 Descriptive Display – teacher notes

ACTIVITY OBJECTIVES

- Children develop responsibility for themselves.
- Children's ability to manage their time is enhanced, for school, family and leisure.
- Children are assisted in planning their time.
- Children have guideposts so they know what is happening and when.
- Children feel secure and calm with the weekly routine – they know what to expect during the weekly schedule.

WORKSHEET REQUIREMENTS

You will need:

- A3 paper
- Pictures/graphics
- Velcro dots
- Laminating device
- Scissors
- Hanging devices (tack, chain or string)
- Non-permanent marker

MAIN ACTIVITY

- Children follow the instructions on the worksheet, resulting in them creating an adaptable, portable timetable. In advance, make as many photocopies as you need of the timetable on p.23 at A3 size.
- The visual timetable can be adapted for both home and school activities.
- Alternatively two timetables can be created, one for home and one for school.

EXTENSION ACTIVITIES

- Working with the children you could create additional schedules, such as recreational schedules, morning/night time schedules, electronic schedules using the computer, and the child's own responsibilities schedule.

2.3 Descriptive Display

This is a timetable for you to use at home or school, or both.

Follow the instructions below to create a timetable that suits you; you can check it each day to see your programme or routine.

- Cut out the timetable from the A3 sheet your helper has given you.

- Ask your helper to laminate the timetable.

- With a non-permanent marker, write your routine for specific days, e.g. Monday is special lesson, Tuesday is dance class, etc., or cut out pictures/graphics and attach them to your schedule with Velcro dots.

- There are two methods of using the timetable. You can fix it to the fridge or on a wall at home or school, or you can attach it to your school bag by a chain or string – it can be hanging outside or inside.

- Schedule can be changed each day if necessary, e.g. to show when you'll have lunch, whether you need your reading book, whether you'll have to bring a note, which textbooks you need, which games you'll play, etc.

Monday	Tuesday	Wednesday	Thursday	Friday

2.4 Systems Schedule – teacher notes

ACTIVITY OBJECTIVES

- Children learn how to prepare daily timetables by subject/time.
- Children break school lessons/work into bite-size chunks that are doable and achievable.
- Children are supported to develop a positive attitude toward school.
- Children learn study management skills.
- Children's self-motivation is enhanced.
- Children learn more about planning their time.

WORKSHEET REQUIREMENTS

You will need:

- Coloured card – you may require up to five different colours, one for each week day
- Scissors
- Laminating device
- Non-permanent marker
- Velcro dots

MAIN ACTIVITY

This activity is to help children keep on schedule with each lesson at school. Following the instructions on the worksheet, they will produce an adaptable schedule to refer to during the school day. Children develop their organisational competencies by breaking each day into separate lessons/segments/tasks. You will need to photocopy the schedule on the worksheet onto five different coloured cards for each child.

EXTENSION ACTIVITIES

- Children either say or draw the steps involved in achieving a home project/task (e.g. putting out the garbage, making their bed, setting the table): 'the first thing I do is…, the second thing I do is…, the third thing I do is…'
- Children colour code subjects in their work folders to help them get more organised. For example, all maths is red, all language is yellow, all sport is orange, etc.
- Homework/project system schedule: children make a plan of what work needs to be completed by what date, and make a mini plan of what is involved in each step of the project (e.g. browse the internet, go to the library).

2.4 Systems Schedule

This activity is to help you keep on schedule with each lesson at school.

Follow the instructions below to create cards that can be placed in your desk, so you can check whenever you are unsure as to what is happening next.

- Cut out the daily schedules.

- Ask your helper to laminate the schedules.

- With a non-permanent marker, write what your daily routine is at school under the specific days, e.g. Monday 9am = maths, 10.30 = break, 11am = science, etc., or cut out pictures/graphics and attach them to your schedule with Velcro dots.

- Place the schedule on or in your desk so you can check it when necessary.

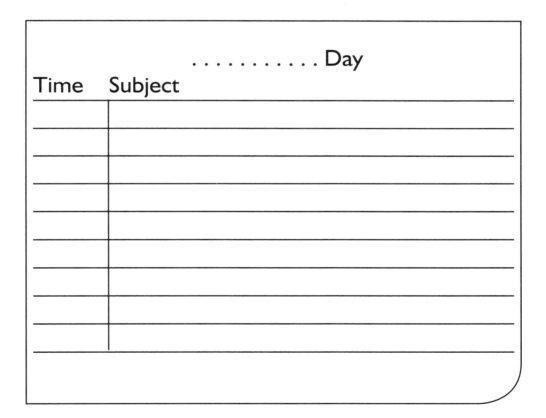

Time	Subject

. . . . Day

2.5 Identification Icons – teacher notes

Note: This activity is more suited to middle and upper primary years.

ACTIVITY OBJECTIVES

Using visual cues as reminders to promote or encourage desired social behaviours:

- Children's attitude to self-motivation and self-discipline will be improved.
- Children will be able to apply themselves to performance situations.
- Children's emphasis on achieving their personal best will increase – 'I can' behaviours.
- Children will focus on effort and personal best.

WORKSHEET REQUIREMENTS

You will need:

- Coloured card
- Scissors
- Laminating device
- Velcro dots

MAIN ACTIVITY

Children use the worksheet to produce a set of icon cards to display as motivational reminder cues on their desktop. They can have a set each or share one set as a group. You will need to photocopy the worksheet onto coloured card.

The cards can be used in several different ways:

- Visual reminders for children to self-monitor.
- For helper to cue/prompt children to focus their attention on specific 'I can' behaviours.
- If the child is non-verbal, the cards can be used as a form of communication.

EXTENSION ACTIVITIES

- Individual children focus on different 'I can' cues.
- Classes/groups of children concentrate on same/different 'I can' cues.
- Children draw their own 'I can' cards.
- Children congratulate their peers using the 'I can' statements.
- Helper enlarges the cards and uses them as visual reminders.

2.5 Identification Icons

This activity is to help you focus so you can be more organised. You can use the icons to remind yourself of some goals or strategies, and also your teacher can use your icons to assist you.

Follow the instructions below to create icon cards that can be placed on your desk so you can see them, to remind yourself to stay focused and be organised.

- Cut out the icons.

- Ask your helper to laminate the icons.

- Attach them to your desk with Velcro dots.

2.6 Methodical Mapping – teacher notes

ACTIVITY OBJECTIVES

- Children will become more organised with their homework, as they are introduced to the concept of a homework plan.

- Children are encouraged to think about their thinking as far as homework is concerned – where, when, what and how homework happens.

- Children apply themselves to study or preparation.

- Children's concentration before/during homework tasks is supported.

- A home environment is created that helps the homework process.

- Children's study skills improve.

- Children are taught that learning happens at home as well as school.

- Children develop independence and responsibility.

- Children's appreciation of homework time and tasks increases.

- Children develop some understanding of their homework style.

- Children learn to manage their time.

- Children can prepare a study homework timetable and follow it.

WORKSHEET REQUIREMENTS

You will need:

- A4 paper

- Pen/pencil

MAIN ACTIVITY

- Children answer the questions on the worksheet to get an idea of their approach to homework.

- Using their responses, and with the help and input of an adult, children can put together a plan that will help them improve their homework approach.

EXTENSION ACTIVITIES

- Children interview family members across the generations to learn more about how they organise themselves for homework, chores, etc.

2.6 Methodical Mapping

This activity is to help you be more organised with your homework. Planning your homework makes you more and organised gives you more free time to do the things you like. Let's find out what you think about homework.

- Read the questions and write the answers down.

- Discuss your answers with an adult.

- Together with that adult work out a homework plan for the week.

- Follow through with the homework plan for the week.

- At the end of the week, discuss any positives/negatives you had with your homework plan with an adult.

- When are homework tasks announced in class?

- Where and when do you write down your homework tasks?

- How often do you do homework?

- Where do you do homework?

- How long does your homework take you?

- At what time do you start your homework?

- When do you finish your homework?

- What do you do if you need help with your homework?

- How do you work out your homework deadlines?

- How do you decide what homework to do first?

- How do you deal with distractions during homework time?

- What do you do once your homework is finished?

- What extra-curricular activities do you do and how do you plan your homework around these activities?

- What free nights do you have during the school week and what do you do during these times?

---

3 Being Persistent – Music Themed

Importance of the capability

Persistence means having staying power: being tenacious, sticking to your position or purpose, trying hard, expending effort and not giving up when something feels like it's too difficult, frustrating, uninteresting or tedious. Children who have learned to be persistent apply themselves to a task; they keep on focusing and trying. They do not give up when things are new or they appear taxing, dull or monotonous. They plan their time, check their work ensuring it is the best they can do, and are willing to put off certain tasks until the task at hand is achieved. They are prepared to do things they do not want to do and to put in the effort to achieve the desired/required outcome.

Persistent behaviour involves planning, hard work, calculated risks, setbacks, effort, commitment, effort, engagement, motivation and determination.

List of activities

3.1 Commitment Cards   –   'I can' statements
3.2 Selfless Service   –   Voluntary service record
3.3 Morning Melody   –   Morning timetable
3.4 Golden Goals   –   Goal setting
3.5 Hard Yakka   –   Thinking plan
3.6 Afternoon Aims   –   Afternoon timetable

3.1 Commitment Cards – teacher notes

Note: This activity is more suited to middle and upper primary years.

ACTIVITY OBJECTIVES

- Children identify positive 'I can' achiever thinking.
- Children learn that people have both strengths and weaknesses and the 'I can' Commitment Cards represent strengths or goals to achieve.
- Children learn that people need to persist with their helpful behaviours if they are to develop their many different qualities and characteristics.
- Children are assisted as they continue to develop their self-acceptance.
- Children relate the 'I can' commitment cards to themselves and to others.

WORKSHEET REQUIREMENTS

You will need:

- Coloured card
- Pen
- Scissors
- Laminating device

MAIN ACTIVITY

- Children create their own Commitment Cards (with positive statements relating to helpful behaviours) using the instructions on the worksheet. The worksheet should be photocopied onto coloured card for this activity.
- Children refer to their Commitment Cards as prompts when they need a reminder of how to be persistent.

EXTENSION ACTIVITIES

- Children design and use a poster that features affirmative 'I can' phrases.
- Children make a pocket-size flip card chart with 'I can' commitment messages.
- Children role-play consequences of persisting with the 'I can' Commitment Cards and resisting them.
- Children make up 'I can' affirmation stories for peers/family members.
- Children invent and play 'I can' memory card games.
- Children design an 'I can' personal advertisement/news flash.
- Children visualise 'I can' events in their school and family life.
- Children mind map all the 'I can' strategies they use to help them function in stressful times.
- Children give themselves – and others – at least three affirmations every day.

3.1 Commitment Cards

This activity is to help you realise how persistent you can become by trying new things and committing to new experiences.

Follow the instructions below to create 12 cards that you can use as 'I can' statements:

- Write in the blank cards things that can help you to be persistent.

- Cut out the cards.

- Ask your helper to laminate the cards.

Now you have a set of commitment cards to help you achieve your goal of being persistent.

I can try new things	I can ask for help	I can put in effort
I can do it!	I can learn	I can be calm
I can follow my plan	I can listen	I can do the hard work

3.2 Selfless Service – teacher notes

ACTIVITY OBJECTIVES

- Children learn the importance of doing something for others without expecting something in return.

- Children receive self-gratification for doing unpaid service for someone else.

- Children experience giving to others without expecting something in return.

WORKSHEET REQUIREMENTS

You will need:

- Coloured card

- Pen

- Scissors

- Laminating device

MAIN ACTIVITY

- Children use the worksheet to create a Voluntary Service Record, with a plan of how they will help their community. You will need to photocopy the worksheet onto coloured card.

- Children engage in voluntary service in the classroom/school community/ local community.

- Children sign and date their Record once they have successfully completed their planned voluntary service.

- If the card is laminated and a non-permanent marker is used, the Record can be re-used again and again.

EXTENSION ACTIVITIES

- Families get involved in community service.

- Children design a poster of community service ideas.

- Children choose a person and do voluntary service for him or her.

- The class/family sponsors a community who are not as privileged as themselves, for example a World Vision child or community.

- Helper invites members of the school/local community who are involved in voluntary service to talk about their roles and responsibilities.

3.2 Selfless Service

Do you perform any voluntary (selfless) service? Voluntary (selfless) service is when you volunteer your time to help someone else. Sometimes it means putting in effort and doing something without being asked. In this activity you record your voluntary (selfless) service for a month.

Follow the instructions below to create your Voluntary Service Record.

- Fill in your plan for voluntary service for the month.

- Cut out the card and ask your helper to laminate it.

- Place it in your diary, on your wall or in your desk at school.

- When you have carried out your voluntary (selfless) service, sign and date your card.

See below for an example.

MY SELFLESS SERVICE FOR THE MONTH OF JUNE	MY SELFLESS SERVICE FOR THE MONTH OF _____
WHO: For Grandpa	WHO:
WHAT: I will water his garden	WHAT:
WHEN: On Saturday	WHEN:
HOW MANY TIMES: Weekly	HOW MANY TIMES:
I performed my selfless service for the month of June.	I performed my selfless service for the month of
My name is Joe Carter	My name is
Date	Date
Signature	Signature

3.3 Morning Melody – teacher notes

ACTIVITY OBJECTIVES

- Children learn to persist with morning tasks in a calm manner.
- Children put in effort as they follow their morning schedule through to the end.
- Children develop more responsibility for getting themselves ready in the morning.
- Children familiarise themselves with pursuing organised tasks in a timely manner.

WORKSHEET REQUIREMENTS

You will need:

- A3 paper/card
- Scissors
- Pictures/graphics
- Laminating device
- Non-permanent marker
- Velcro dots

MAIN ACTIVITY

- Children think about the tasks that happen in the morning and sequence them.
- Using the worksheet (photocopied to A3 size), and with assistance from their helper, children sequence these tasks, resulting in the creation of their own personal schedule, which can be used for home and/or school.

EXTENSION ACTIVITIES

- Children create a class/family chart of morning tasks showing, for example, what happens in each family between the hours of 7am and 9am: e.g. Dad leaves for the gym at 7am and is at work at 8am; Mum is making breakfast at 7am, etc.
- Children add 'Feelings' words/symbols to the tasks in the schedule (using a Velcro dot) to show how they are feeling about the task that day.
- Children formulate schedules for other parts of the day, using words and pictures.
- Helper takes photographs of children completing each mini task involved in morning schedule.
- Children draw pictures of persisting with tasks named in the morning schedule.
- Children include the time when tasks are to be completed by in the morning schedule.
- Children make 'To Do' lists for the morning and cross out tasks as they are completed.

3.3 Morning Melody

This is a morning timetable for you to use at home so you can stay focused and help your morning go smoothly.

Follow the instructions below to create a timetable that suits you. You can check it each morning to see your routine for the day:

- Cut out the timetable below.

- Draw/cut out pictures of what the chore looks like.

- Ask your helper to laminate the timetable.

- Fix it to a wall in your home, on the fridge or at school.

- With a non-permanent marker put a tick or a smiley face in the right box when you accomplish a task, and put a cross or a sad face when you don't manage it.

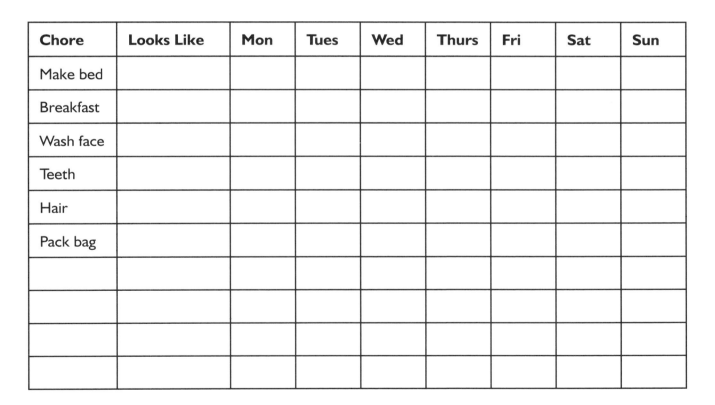

Chore	Looks Like	Mon	Tues	Wed	Thurs	Fri	Sat	Sun
Make bed								
Breakfast								
Wash face								
Teeth								
Hair								
Pack bag								

3.4 Golden Goals – teacher notes

ACTIVITY OBJECTIVES

- Children learn that doing their best, persisting with goals, regardless of the final outcome, is important.

- Children recognise the importance of personal goal setting.

- Children persevere in order to achieve their personal goals.

- Children learn the difference between giving up on their personal goals and sticking with their plan to achieve these goals.

WORKSHEET REQUIREMENTS

You will need:

- A4 or A3 card or paper

- Scissors

- Pen/pencil

- Pictures/graphics

- Hanging device

MAIN ACTIVITY

- Children set personal and academic goals on a daily/weekly basis.

- Children create a 'Golden Goal' using the worksheet (at A4 or A3 size) to help them keep on track with their goals and celebrate meeting them.

EXTENSION ACTIVITIES

- Children design a flow chart showing the outcomes of persisting with goal attainment and of giving up on goal attainment.

- Children make a personal goal-setting target board. It should be designed in the shape and style of an archery target board and decorated with visual reminders of children's personal goals.

- Children visualise achieving goals.

- Children set immediate, short-term and long-term goals for themselves.

- Children and adults set goals together as a family unit.

3.4 Golden Goals

Having goals can help you achieve the things you want to do. Goals can help you stay focused so you don't give up too easily.

We have created a 'Golden Goal' below for you to complete. Together with your helper, work out what you would like some help with, whether it be behaviour or an achievement, and set your goal.

- Cut out the blank 'Golden Goal' below.

- Fill in the blanks.

- Draw/cut out pictures of what your goal looks like.

- Fix it to a wall in your home, on the fridge or at school.

My goal is . . . .

Because . . . .

Some things I intend to do to reach my goal include . . . .

. . . .

. . . .

I will strive to reach my goal by . . . .

. . . .

The help I might need in reaching my goal is . . . .

. . . .

. . . .

When I achieve my goal I will . . . .

. . . .

Picture/s of me achieving my goal

3.5 Hard Yakka – teacher notes

ACTIVITY OBJECTIVES

- Children are aware of the thinking component of behaviour.
- Children learn to differentiate between helpful and unhelpful thinking.
- Children are supported as they learn the hard yakka (an Australian word meaning 'work') associated with helpful thinking.
- Children recognise that thinking behaviour is a choice.
- Children identify examples of unhelpful and helpful thinking.
- Children learn that some thinking helps and other thinking hinders.
- Children learn that the decisions they make have consequences.
- Children recognise that people can think differently about the same event.

WORKSHEET REQUIREMENTS

You will need:

- A4 paper
- Pen/pencil
- Scissors

MAIN ACTIVITY

- Children think about helpful thinking statements for school/family life events.
- Children use the worksheet to journal their own happening–thinking–doing life stories.

EXTENSION ACTIVITIES

- Children role-play the helpful thinking and unhelpful thinking segment of the happening–thinking–doing sequence.
- Children write their own helpful thinking phrases in speech bubbles for familiar characters in stories.
- Children design comics with helpful and unhelpful thinking bubbles.
- Children compare their thinking bubble comics.

3.5 Hard Yakka

Sometimes we have to put in the 'hard yakka' (an Australian phrase meaning 'hard work') to get through something that challenges us. When something happens, our thoughts help us to decide what to do. Look below at some helpful and unhelpful thinking.

There are two scenarios. See if you can come up with another one.

- Read through the scenarios in the chart below.

- Mind map your responses to the first two 'happenings'.

- Make up another 'Happening' scenario and fill in the blanks.

- Cut out your completed 'Hard Yakka' activity.

Happening	Thinking	Doing
Homework is challenging	I give up I can ask for help I can't do it Even though it's hard, I'll give it a go	Make a start Ask for help
Your friends are playing a new game that you've never played before	Learning something new can be fun I dont want to play a new game I'll give it a go I won't be any good at it	Listening to learn Joining in

3.6 Afternoon Aims – teacher notes

ACTIVITY OBJECTIVES

- Children follow the afternoon schedule as outlined.
- Children persist with their afternoon tasks in a calm manner.
- Children put in effort as they follow their afternoon schedule in a timely manner.
- Children develop responsibility for their afternoon routine.
- Children familiarise themselves with pursuing organised tasks in timely manner.

WORKSHEET REQUIREMENTS

You will need:

- A3 paper/card
- Pen/pencil
- Scissors
- Pictures/graphics
- Laminating device
- Non-permanent marker
- Hanging device or Velcro dots

MAIN ACTIVITY

- Children create a schedule using the worksheet (which should be photocopied onto A3 size paper) and contribute information so the schedule can be completed and signed off.
- Children can time themselves following through with their afternoon schedule.

EXTENSION ACTIVITIES

- Helper creates a 'Catch them in the act' afternoon schedule picture board with photographs of children persisting with and completing schedule tasks.
- Children compare afternoon schedules for school days, weekends and holidays.
- Children strive to beat the previous times set for completing tasks named on their afternoon schedule.
- Children differentiate between what are the most important and least important tasks on their schedule, and compare and contrast their priority list with family members.

3.6 Afternoon Aims

This is an afternoon timetable for you to use at home so you can stay focused and help your afternoons go smoothly.

Follow the instructions below to create a timetable that suits you. You can check it each afternoon to see your routine for the day:

- Cut out the timetable below.

- Draw/cut out pictures of what the chore looks like.

- Ask your helper to laminate the timetable.

- With a non-permanent marker, put a tick or a smiley face in the right box when you accomplish a task, and put a cross or a sad face when you don't manage it.

- Fix it to a wall in your home or school, or on the fridge.

Chore	Looks Like	Mon	Tues	Wed	Thurs	Fri	Sat	Sun
Wash hands								
Get changed								
Unpack								
Snack								
Relax								
Exercise								
Chores/Pets								
Shower/Bath								
Dinner								
Bedtime								

4 Becoming Confident – Numeracy Themed

SUCCESS

Importance of the capability

Children who have learned to be confident believe in their own self-worth, maintain a positive view of themselves and have faith in their abilities. They have an 'I can do it' attitude, are willing to try new activities and to ask for help when they need it. They are not worried or afraid about making mistakes or trying something new, challenging or complex. Confident children believe they will be successful if they try hard. They are willing to try something new even though they might not be able to do it first time. They are risk takers and recognise that it is okay to make mistakes and that mistakes are part of learning. They try their very best, and trust in themselves, their abilities and capabilities. They are self-reliant and also willing to participate in a wide range of activities. Children who have learned to be confident are solution finders – they don't dwell on problems. They think positively about themselves when things are not going their way. They stand up for themselves when the situation demands. They are independent, self-assured, self-reliant and composed.

List of activities

4.1 Positive Panels	–	Confidence identifier
4.2 Quantum of Qualities	–	Personal identifier
4.3 What Do I Do?	–	Task analysis
4.4 Wise Words	–	Social script
4.5 Success Scales	–	Sentence starters
4.6 Me-tathlon	–	Autobiography

4.1 Positive Panels – teacher notes

ACTIVITY OBJECTIVES

- Children deepen their understanding of confidence booster and confidence destroyer phrases.

- Children think about their own language – does it boost or put down their confidence?

- Children think about their own self-talk – does it boost or put them down?

- Children are more aware of the link between booster self-talk and a confident self-image and self-concept.

WORKSHEET REQUIREMENTS

You will need:

- White A4 paper

- Green and red markers/crayons/pencils

- Scissors

MAIN ACTIVITY

- Children colour the confidence booster phrases on the worksheet in shades of green and the put downs in shades of red.

- Children give real-life examples of behaviours associated with the nominated Positive Panels.

- Children refer to the Positive Panels and create both a generic and personal confidence wall with booster phrases.

- Children act out the impact of confidence boosters and put downs.

- Children move to music that inspires confidence booster thinking.

- Children take turns providing antidotes to put downs.

- Children find their own confident qualities according to scripts.

- Children tell stories sharing the reasons behind their choice of confident scripts.

EXTENSION ACTIVITIES

- Helper sets up a daily ritual at home and school where children can give one another confidence boosters.

- Children listen to their self-talk – do they give themselves confidence boosters or destroyer put downs?

- Helper catches children in the act of giving confidence boosters to self and others.

- Children can reinterpret scenes from fairy tales using booster and put-down language.

- Children play a game of charades, acting out booster phrases.

- Children count the number of confidence phrases they say out loud or in their head.

- Children interview family members about their confident acts.

- Children catch others in the act of performing confidence tasks.

- Children celebrate 'have a go' behaviours in self and others.

- Children set themselves a goal of confident behaviours.

4.1 Positive Panels

To help build your confidence, it is important to think and feel positive.

- Read each panel and decide which ones boost your confidence, and which ones destroy your confidence.

- Colour the panels that boost your confidence GREEN.

- Colour the panels that destroy your confidence RED.

- Cut out the panels and discuss them further with your peers or adult helper.

M + E
= ME

A boy called me an idiot.	I have a great sense of humour.	Teacher congratulated me on my project.
I completed my morning timetable all by myself.	I tripped over, got up and kept going.	My friend said I played fair.
A girl told others stories about me that were not true.	I'm proud to be me.	I'm dumb at sport.

4.2 Quantum of Qualities – teacher notes

ACTIVITY OBJECTIVES

- Children reflect on and identify their personal qualities.
- Children are proud of their gifts and their distinctiveness.
- Children like what they see when they think about who they are.
- Children develop respect for themselves and their exceptional abilities.

WORKSHEET REQUIREMENTS

You will need:

- A4 paper
- Pen/pencil
- Dictionary/thesaurus

MAIN ACTIVITY

- Using the worksheet and a dictionary/thesaurus, children investigate the meanings of different personal qualities.
- Children think about and mind map the personal qualities of themselves and others. They then think about and discuss how their own unique mix of qualities makes them who they are.

EXTENSION ACTIVITIES

- Children do a project on personal qualities.
- Children make a personal qualities 'ME' badge.
- Children talk about a time when their personal qualities came to the fore.
- Children mind map character qualities.
- Children identify personal qualities in others.
- Children think about their own personal qualities.
- Children make a mobile of nominated personal qualities.
- Children create a personal qualities crossword.
- Children write lyrics to a familiar tune using words from their personal qualities list.
- Children keep a journal of their daily interactions with peers and identify what qualities they demonstrated in different play episodes.

4.2 Quantum of Qualities

- Look through the list of qualities below. If you don't know what some of them mean, look them up in a dictionary or ask your adult helper.

- Choose five qualities that are 'just you' and list them.

- Give reasons for your choices.

- Combine all the qualities together and you have your personal identity profile.

- Discuss this with your peers or adult helper.

LOYAL	FRIENDLY	HELPFUL
KIND	PROUD	RELIABLE
TRUSTWORTHY	RESPECTFUL	RESPONSIBLE
CARING	HONEST	DETERMINED
FAIR	PATIENT	COURAGEOUS
CONSIDERATE	CONFIDENT	

1. ……………….…because…………………………………………………

2. ……………….…because…………………………………………………

3. ……………….…because……………………….…………………………

4. ……………….…because……………………….…………………………

5. ……………….…because…………………………………………………

= ME!

4.3 What Do I Do? – teacher notes

ACTIVITY OBJECTIVES

- Children learn the importance of following each step in a particular sequence to reach a successful outcome.

- Children learn more about the importance of having a plan about what to do when certain situations arise so that they remain calm, confident and in control.

- Children develop their confidence in following through with a particular sequence to achieve a desired result.

WORKSHEET REQUIREMENTS

You will need:

- A4 or A3 paper

- Magazines/computer graphics

- Pen/pencil

- Scissors

MAIN ACTIVITY

- Children work closely with their helper to choose a situation they need help with and create a story to help them decide on an approach.

- By filling in the worksheet they create a visual guide to help them every time they encounter that situation.

- *Example*: if the situation were 'What do I do to catch the bus?' children could write the following sentences down the right-hand column of the table: 'I wait for my bus. It is No. 75.'; 'When I see the bus I put out my hand to hail it.'; 'I step onto the bus and give the driver my ticket/money.'; and 'I sit in a seat near to the front.' They would then draw a suitable picture in the left-hand box next to each instruction.

EXTENSION ACTIVITIES

- Children think about the animal kingdom and talk about what different types of animal would do if other animals moved into their territory. They then act out these imaginary scenarios.

- Children talk about what to do when out-of-the-ordinary social situations occur. They come up with three to five suggestions and then debate the pros and cons of each solution.

- Children compile a 'what to do when' task analysis of everyday situations – they personalise them for different family members and peers.

4.3 What Do I Do?

You can create your own step-by-step personalised story when you are unsure as to what to do in a particular social or emotional situation, such as what to do when you are feeling angry or what to do at the school swimming carnival. Knowing what to do and being prepared gives you confidence. Together with your adult helper, choose a situation that you need some assistance with, and create a 'What do I do when?' story below to help you through that situation next time.

You can draw or cut out pictures for the graphic box (on the left) and write step-by-step instructions in the text box (on the right).

What I do when	

4.4 Wise Words – teacher notes

ACTIVITY OBJECTIVES

- Children are introduced to assertive phrases to say when faced with difficult/unfamiliar/new situations.

- Children learn that there is more than one script response to the same social situation.

- Children familiarise themselves with more than one social script for the same social situation – when one script does not work they can use another script for the same situation.

WORKSHEET REQUIREMENTS

You will need:

- A4 paper
- Pen/pencil
- Scissors

MAIN ACTIVITY

- Children fill in the worksheet with their own examples of appropriate 'wise words' for given situations.

- Subsequent discussion and role-play may consist of the following:

  - Children think about different social situations where wise assertive words would be helpful – in the classroom (e.g. asking for help with school work); in the playground (joining in a game); outside school hours care (e.g. waiting for a turn on computer); at home (e.g. asking a sibling to stay out of your bedroom); visiting friends, etc.

  - Children write down a possible assertive phrase to say for three different situations.

  - Helper models the different responses to the identified social situations.

  - Children role-play.

  - Children record the phrases on business card-size cardboard.

  - Children use the phrases when the situation arises.

EXTENSION ACTIVITIES

- Children create a 'Big Book' of assertive phrase responses to identified social situations.

- Children personalise the 'Big Book' into a mini book for themselves.

- Children compare and contrast their 'what to say' social scripts.

- Children suggest additional assertive phrases for peers' 'what to say' situations.

- Children compile a 'what to say when…' social script book for younger children.

- Children illustrate the 'what to say' scripts reflecting the cultures of the class group.

- Children classify the 'what to say' scripts across different social contexts.

4.4 Wise Words

Do you sometimes not know what to say when you are playing? If you are confident, wise words will be easier for you.

Below are three scenarios. We have provided you with some appropriate wise words and there is room for you to add two more examples of other appropriate wise words you can say.

When you have finished, cut out the scenarios and discuss and role-play with your peers or adult helper.

When someone is annoying you:

Say 'Leave me alone'   or   'I'm getting mad!'

Or .... Or ....

When someone pushes in line:

Say 'Wait your turn'   or   'It's my turn, not yours!'

Or .... Or ....

When someone says you can't join in the game:

Say 'OK, I'll start my own game'   or   'When can I join in?'

Or .... Or ....

4.5 Success Scales – teacher notes

ACTIVITY OBJECTIVES

- Children learn to differentiate between helpful and unhelpful behaviours.

- Children are supported as they learn helpful ways of responding to situations.

- Children recognise that their behaviour is chosen – their preferred choice at the time is not necessarily the most appropriate choice.

- Children identify examples of unhelpful and helpful thinking, feeling and doing.

- Children learn there are consequences for the decisions they make.

- Children recognise that people may think differently about the same event.

- Children begin to understand/deepen their understanding that some thinking helps (positive thinking) and other thinking hinders (negative thinking).

WORKSHEET REQUIREMENTS

You will need:

- A4 paper

- Pen/pencil

MAIN ACTIVITY

- Prior to completing the worksheet, children mind map emotional responses to the successes and difficulties they experience. For example: 'being great at maths makes me feel proud' or 'finding handwriting difficult makes me feel frustrated'.

- Children work in teams with one team naming positive/helpful strategies in response to social scenarios and the second team naming negative/unhelpful strategies in response to the same scenario.

- Children complete the worksheet activity and discuss their responses.

- Children in each team suggest additional strategies to the other team.

EXTENSION ACTIVITIES

- Children make up social scenario strategy card games using emotion faces rather than words.

- Children draw the scenario as a comic strip, adding a social context and characters. Each character in the comic should have talking and thinking bubbles.

- Children conduct a survey of their peers' response strategies.

- Children predict what might happen if a child's response was…compared with…

- Children make two lists. In list A they include positive confident thinking phrases and in list B they include negative put down thinking phrases.

- Children talk about each of the social situations named in the activity.

- Children mind map different ways of responding to these situations.

- Children choose strategies relevant to themselves.

- Children chat about their nominated strategies.

- Children act out their chosen strategies.

4.5 Success Scales

Sometimes we can have lots of mixed emotions about trying something new. If you are confident within yourself, then these things become easier to do and you will feel successful.

Below are some scenarios where you might have a positive or a negative emotion.

Choose an emotion to go with the scenario, and then a strategy – we have provided some suggested strategies to choose from.

SUCCESS

PRACTISE WHAT TO SAY	BREATHE IN, BREATHE OUT
PRACTISE MY SPELLING	RING UP AND ASK
WATCH FIRST THEN ASK TO PLAY	SPEAK WITH CONFIDENCE
WAIT MY TURN AND JOIN IN	TRY MY HARDEST
THINK, 'ASKING FOR HELP IS WISE'	CHOOSE TO HAVE FUN
THINK, 'ASKING FOR HELP WILL HELP ME'	GO WITH A FRIEND

I am worried/calm about the spelling test.

My strategy is ....

I am afraid/fearless about joining in a game.

My strategy is ....

I am unsure/confident about going to a birthday party.

My strategy is ....

I am scared/prepared to ask for help.

My strategy is ....

I am anxious/happy talking to the class.

My strategy is ....

I am nervous/brave when ringing up a friend.

My strategy is ....

4.6 Me-tathlon – teacher notes

ACTIVITY OBJECTIVES

- Children get to know themselves a little better.
- Children develop a deeper appreciation of who they are.
- Children provide information about themselves.
- Children identify their own unique qualities and the unique qualities of others.

WORKSHEET REQUIREMENTS

You will need:

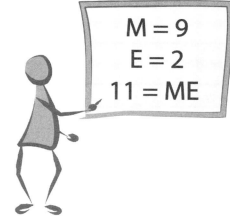

- A4 paper
- Pen/pencil

MAIN ACTIVITY

- Children work with a partner – one child records their peer's responses to each Me-tathlon worksheet question.
- Children share their Me-tathlon responses with the class group.
- Children make up a Me-tathlon secret code for family members, using each letter in 'Me-tathlon' to begin the name of a quality their family member has.

EXTENSION ACTIVITIES

- Children compare and contrast their Me-tathlon responses with their peers.
- Children interview different family members, young and old, and complete their Me-tathlon.
- Children set up special interest groups based on Me-tathlon responses.
- Children compile a newspaper advertisement promoting their Me-tathlon qualities.

4.6 Me-tathlon

If you are proud of who you are, then you will be a confident person. What are the interesting things about you? What makes you an interesting person? Fill out the 'Me-tathlon' below and share with your peers and adult helper.

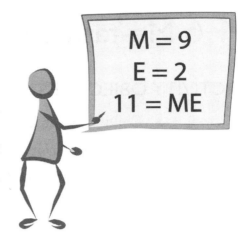

Me!		How I look	
My name is		I look special because	
I live at			
I am years old		My eyes are	
I was born on		My hair is	
My nickname is		What I love about the way I look is	
My friends		**Favourite things**	
My best friend is		Foods	
Because		Music	
		Colour	
My other friends are		Book	
		Movie	
		Radio station	
		TV show	
		Sport	
My school		**My special interests**	
My teacher's name is		In my free time I like to	
My favourite subject is		I'm really good at	
At lunchtimes I			
		I sit next to	

5 Sociability – Creative Arts Themed

Importance of the capability

Sociability is about being companionable and ready and disposed to engage in mutual interaction. Children who have learned to be sociable demonstrate understanding, friendliness, adaptability, empathy and politeness in group settings. It is about collaborating in small groups, working within social guidelines and playing nicely and being friendly. Sociability is about getting along with others, working well with peers, being thoughtful and compassionate. It involves solving social problems without getting infuriated.

Sociable children are happy and joy-filled. They have positive peer and adult–child relationships. They get along with others. They cooperate with and listen to one another, are interested in helping others and have appropriate friendship skills and competencies.

Children's relationships with others are of central importance to their development.

List of activities

5.1 Play Planner   –   Play choice chart

5.2 Friendship Facts –   Sentence starters

5.3 Charm Cards   –   Compliment cards

5.4 Roving Reporter   –   Listening and recording

5.5 Cube Chat   –   Interest identifier

5.6 Buddy Bookmark   –   Personal descriptor

5.1 Play Planner – teacher notes

ACTIVITY OBJECTIVES

- Children learn how to plan their play dates.
- Children decide what, with whom and when they will involve themselves in play opportunities.
- Children become more relaxed and confident when it comes to play time activities.
- Children take more responsibility for their play.
- Children become confident with play date plans.

WORKSHEET REQUIREMENTS

You will need:

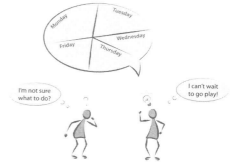

- Paper/card (coloured if preferred)
- Markers, crayons, pencils, glue, glitter

MAIN ACTIVITY

- Using the worksheet (which can be enlarged or reduced to suit your needs) children plan what to do for a play date to happen – before, during and after the play date. (After the play date children could write a letter or SMS to their peer to say thank you.)
- Children use their completed Play Planner to organise themselves so the play date is fun.
- Children work out 'what to do' plans for when/if something does not go to plan during the play date.

EXTENSION ACTIVITIES

- Play date plans can be modified for planning other social activities through the week.

5.1 Play Planner

To help you plan your free time, we have provided below a Play Planner for you to complete and keep for reference.

- With your helper, fill in the spaces on the Play Planner for each day with what/where you can play that day.

- Decorate your Play Planner.

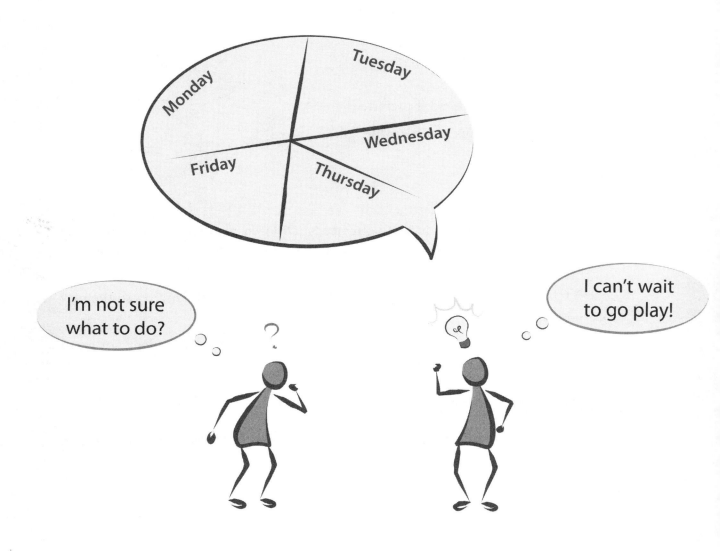

5.2 Friendship Facts – teacher notes

ACTIVITY OBJECTIVES

- Children are aware of friendly behaviour.

- Children understand the differences between true blue and fair weather friendships.

- Helper discusses with children the value of true blue friendship – what a friend is and how friends behave with one another.

- Children's understanding of and appreciation for friendship (true blue and fair weather) is broadened.

WORKSHEET REQUIREMENTS

You will need:

- A4 paper

- Pen/pencil

MAIN ACTIVITY

- Children compare and contrast their own responses on the Friendship Facts interview worksheet with their peers' responses.

- Children classify this information into two distinct groups: true blue friend and fair weather friend.

- Children hypothesise what will happen if/when certain friendly actions happen/do not happen.

- Children design a poster advertising true blue friendship.

EXTENSION ACTIVITIES

- Children formulate a friendship formula naming all the characteristics of friendly behaviours.

- Children design a comic showing examples of the qualities and actions of true blue friends.

- Children use the elements of the friendship formula to make up a true blue friendship chant.

5.2 Friendship Facts

Are you a social person? Do you make friends easily? Let's learn a little more about your friends, your friendships and your friendship skills.

Below are some questions that may help you learn about your gifts and challenges in the area of friendship. Fill in the blanks with your answers.

My Friends

My friends are [what are the names of your friends?]

....

....

My friends and I [what are some of the things you and your friends do together?]

....

....

I make new friends by [what skills do you use to introduce yourself to a new person to become their friend?]

....

....

I keep my friends by

....

....

I value my friends because

....

....

I choose my friends because [why do you choose a specific person to be your friend?]

....

....

I'm a true blue friend when [what are the things you do to be a true blue friend?]

....

....

I stay away from fair weather friends because

....

....

My friends like me because [what are some of the qualities that your friends like about you?]

....

....

5.3 Charm Cards – teacher notes

ACTIVITY OBJECTIVES

- Children are aware of what constitutes a kind deed.
- Children acknowledge peers for acts of kindness.
- Children pat themselves on the back, affirming themselves for doing a kind deed.

WORKSHEET REQUIREMENTS

You will need:

- Paper/card (coloured if preferred)
- Pen/pencil
- Scissors

MAIN ACTIVITY

- Children fill out the Charm Cards on the worksheet in recognition of kind acts by peers or helpers witnessed through the day.
- Children acknowledge the kind acts of family members and complete a Charm Card for them.
- Children discuss the value of true blue friendship, what a friend is and how friends behave with one another with their helper/peers.

EXTENSION ACTIVITIES

- Children compile a kind acts inventory for home and school.
- Helper catches children and peers 'in the act' of kind acts.
- Children design a kind acts billboard.
- Children carry out kind acts without expecting something in return.
- Children keep a record of the Charm Cards they receive and the Charm Cards they voluntarily give to others.

5.3 Charm Cards

Isn't it nice to receive compliments? It is also nice to give compliments. Today you will give three different people a compliment.

At the end of the day you will discuss with your helper/peers whether it was easy/hard to find things to compliment, how it felt to give the compliments and also how it felt to receive a compliment (if you received any).

Follow your helper's instructions on how to complete the Charm Cards.

CHARM CARD

Congratulations . . . .

I noticed . . . .

. . . .

Signed . . . .

CHARM CARD

Congratulations . . . .

I noticed . . . .

. . . .

Signed . . . .

CHARM CARD

Congratulations . . . .

I noticed . . . .

. . . .

Signed . . . .

5.4 Roving Reporter – teacher notes

ACTIVITY OBJECTIVES

- Children get to know other children better.

- Children take time to learn a little more about their peers by listening to their stories of friendly behaviours.

- Children learn more about other people by asking them questions, listening to their responses and recording them.

- Children learn the importance of listening when communicating with others.

WORKSHEET REQUIREMENTS

You will need:

- A4 paper

- Pen/pencil

MAIN ACTIVITY

- Children complete the Roving Reporter worksheet and discuss their own and their peers' responses to the interview questions.

- Children identify similarities and differences in these responses.

- Children write a newsletter report with an introduction, body and conclusion based on the information they collected in their interview.

EXTENSION ACTIVITIES

- Children record all the characteristics and qualities listed during the interviews on a large piece of paper fixed to the wall.

- Children predict what might happen when someone chooses friendly as opposed to unfriendly actions.

- Children interview someone older or younger and report on their responses.

5.4 Roving Reporter

To be sociable means to give and take when it comes to speaking and listening. Doing this activity below will help you learn many skills, for example interviewing, listening, recording and writing.

Pair up with a peer and interview each other using the questions below. Listen carefully to their answers and record them below. Using the information recorded on your sheet, write a short report about your peer and read it to the class/group.

What is your best friendly character quality?

....

....

....

What makes you a true blue friend?

....

....

....

What acts of kindness have you done recently at school and at home?

....

....

....

What great achievement have you accomplished with a friend?

....

....

....

✓

If someone has difficulty making new friends, what do you suggest they do?

....

....

....

What friendship quality do you have that you are most proud of?

....

....

....

REPORT

....

....

....

....

....

....

5.5 Cube Chat – teacher notes

ACTIVITY OBJECTIVES

- Children learn more about their peer group by asking them deliberate (always respectful) questions.

- Children learn more about the similarities and differences among people – 'same, same but different'.

- Children realise that people are made up of many qualities, interests, strengths, etc., and this is what makes them unique.

- Children acknowledge that people are different.

WORKSHEET REQUIREMENTS

You will need:

- A4 paper

- Pen/pencil

MAIN ACTIVITY

- Children use the worksheet to find out about the interests and habits of their peers. They record raw data onto the chart provided.

- Children design a tally of responses and calculate the average number of categories per person and the average number of people per category.

- Children discuss, compare and contrast their findings.

EXTENSION ACTIVITIES

- Children ask another class in their school to complete the Cube Chat and then compare these responses with the responses of their own class.

- Children paint or collage a poster capturing their own responses, and cut it into pieces to create a jigsaw puzzle.

- Children design a variation Cube Chat for home.

- Children ask family members to respond to their Cube Chat questions.

5.5 Cube Chat

People like and dislike different things, but they can still have other interests in common. This is what gives us our different identities.

The Cube Chat below will help you find out more about yourself, your peers, your interests and your likes/dislikes.

Write your name into the squares that describe you, then discuss with others the different descriptions in the squares. If someone matches a square, write their name in it. See how many people have similar interests to you.

likes Asian food	has many friends	the youngest in the family
plays a musical instrument	has travelled on an aeroplane	walks/cycles to school
grandparents/aunts and uncles live far away	loves reading books	hand writes letters/ invitations
speaks a second language	does chores at home	plays sport outside of school
tries hard with school work	can fly a kite	has been camping
can count backwards from 1000	learned something new this week	is willing to try new things

5.6 Buddy Bookmark – teacher notes

ACTIVITY OBJECTIVES

- Children identify character strengths and qualities of themselves and their peers.
- Children think more about the qualities of others.
- Children start to broaden their friendship circle.
- Children get to know other children a little better.

WORKSHEET REQUIREMENTS

You will need:

- Paper/card (coloured if preferred)
- Pen/pencil
- Scissors
- Hat or object to put names into
- Glitter, glue, ink pad and stamps for decorating

MAIN ACTIVITY

- Children mind map words for the Buddy Bookmark on the worksheet.
- Children complete the Buddy Bookmark for a peer by writing an acrostic poem using the peer's name.
- Children decorate their Buddy Bookmark before giving it to their peer.
- Children give their Buddy Bookmark at a friendship ceremony.

EXTENSION ACTIVITIES

- Children make a Buddy Bookmark for themselves.
- Children make a Buddy Bookmark for an extended family member, such as a grandparent, aunt or cousin.
- Children give someone who supports them with their learning a Buddy Bookmark, for example, school officer, tutor.

5.6 Buddy Bookmark

Learning more about your buddy can make you both more sociable with one another.

You and your peers will all put their names into a 'hat' – pull a name out and write an acrostic poem about that person using the letters of their name, for example B – Bold, E – Energetic, N – Neat. What you write needs to reflect the character traits and qualities of the other person. It should be positive and reflect true blue friendship.

Decorate the bookmark, show it to your adult helper/class and present it to the friend whose name you used.

6 Regulating Emotions – Sports Themed

My feelings are up in the air

Importance of the capability

Regulating emotions is about being in control and believing in your ability to work through setbacks and risk situations in a capable, effective manner. It is the ability to take a punch emotionally and bounce back from daily challenges.

Children who learn to become resilient are able to deal with life's setbacks and rebound even stronger than before. They cope well with difficulties and with the unexpected, are flexible in outlook, confident, persistent and reflective in action. In a crisis they are able to maintain a sense of calm and optimism, enabling them to handle crisis situations. They expect to find a way to have things turn out well.

This capacity for resilience empowers children to develop personal power and positive self-esteem.

List of activities

6.1 Terrific Target   –   Emotion regulator
6.2 Forensic Feelings   –   Research project
6.3 Empty Emotions   –   Expressing emotions
6.4 Dear Diary   –   Emotions diary
6.5 Extended Emotions   –   Emotion scale
6.6 Merry Medals   –   Descriptive emotions

6.1 Terrific Target – teacher notes

ACTIVITY OBJECTIVES

- Children connect head and heart with emotion regulation.
- Children create and refer to their Terrific Target book to support them, and to calm and relax their mind and body when emotions are beginning to escalate/have escalated.
- Children learn about the importance of calming head and heart when their emotions are beginning to escalate/have escalated.
- Children learn healthy and helpful ways of regulating their own emotions.

WORKSHEET REQUIREMENTS

You will need:

- A4 paper
- Blank exercise book
- Pictures/graphics, e.g. from magazines
- Scissors
- Glue
- Colouring pens/pencils

MAIN ACTIVITY

- Children think about or mind map ideas for their Terrific Target book.
- Children survey family members for ideas to include in their Terrific Target book.
- Children create a Terrific Target book using the instructions on the worksheet. They can refer to it whenever they need to control negative emotions.

EXTENSION ACTIVITIES

- Children compare and contrast their Terrific Target books.
- Children record a tally of how frequently they referred to their Terrific Target book for emotion regulation.
- Children paint self-calming scenes for their Terrific Target book.

6.1 Terrific Target

Sometimes you may have a negative emotion that you are unable to control. You can use your Terrific Target book to help regulate your emotion, to bring it down to a calmer state.

Make and decorate your own Terrific Target book for these kinds of situations. Glue a piece of A4 paper over the front and back of a blank exercise book. Cut out the image below to use on the front of your book. Inside the book, draw or stick in images and words relating to things that make you cheerful. When you start to feel negative emotions, take out your Terrific Target book and browse the images and words that make you feel at peace and happy.

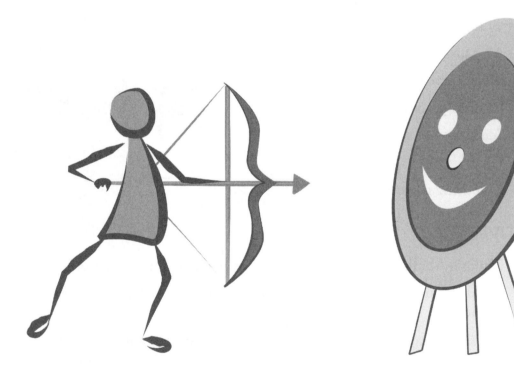

6.2 Forensic Feelings – teacher notes

ACTIVITY OBJECTIVES

- Children think about and identify personal responses to different primary feelings.

- Children expand their emotion literacy by naming different words for the same feelings.

- Children discuss different feelings and ways of expressing these feelings.

- Children learn about helpful ways of expressing their feelings.

WORKSHEET REQUIREMENTS

You will need:

- A4 paper

- Pen/pencil

Breathe calmly

MAIN ACTIVITY

- Children use the worksheet to log their reactions when they experience different emotions.

- When they have completed the example emotions provided, children can research different words to refer to the same emotions.

EXTENSION ACTIVITIES

- Children compile a class A–Z Forensic Feelings book. The first page will contain all the Forensic Feelings information for emotions beginning with 'A', the second page will be 'B', etc.

- Children illustrate 'opposite' emotions from the emotions named, for example, happy–sad; scared–excited.

- Children make a wordsearch with peers' emotion words/ideas.

6.2 Forensic Feelings

Sometimes it can be confusing when we are full of an emotion. We don't know what to do with these feelings.

Below we have provided you with an example of the emotion ANGER.

Fill in the other boxes to help you work out what you can do when you are feeling those emotions.

Example:

Emotion = ANGER   Other words = MAD, FURIOUS, ANNOYED, CROSS

When I'm feeling ANGRY my body = TENSE

What I might be thinking when I'm ANGRY = It's not fair!

What I might be doing when I'm ANGRY = clenching my fists

What I can do and think when I'm feeling ANGRY = breathe calmly, move away

---

Emotion = SADNESS   Other words =

When I'm feeling SAD, my body =

What I might be thinking when I'm SAD =

What I might be doing when I'm SAD =

What I can do and think when I'm feeling SAD =

Emotion = HAPPINESS   Other words =

When I'm feeling HAPPY, my body =

What I might be thinking when I'm HAPPY =

What I might be doing when I'm HAPPY =

What I can do and think when I'm feeling HAPPY =

Emotion = SURPRISE   Other words =

When I'm feeling SURPRISED, my body =

What I might be thinking when I'm SURPRISED =

What I might be doing when I'm SURPRISED =

What I can do and think when I'm feeling SURPRISED =

Emotion = UPSET   Other words =

When I'm feeling UPSET, my body =

What I might be thinking when I'm UPSET =

What I might be doing when I'm UPSET =

What I can do and think when I'm feeling UPSET =

6.3 Empty Emotions – teacher notes

ACTIVITY OBJECTIVES

- Children match feeling words with facial expressions.

- Children learn the language to describe certain emotions.

- Children begin to associate thinking with feelings.

- Children tell stories about social situations when they experienced different feelings.

WORKSHEET REQUIREMENTS

You will need:

- A4 paper

- Pen/pencil

- CD player

MAIN ACTIVITY

- Children use the word puzzles on the worksheet to explore how people express different emotions.

- Children use speaking, writing and drawing to share times when they experienced certain emotions.

EXTENSION ACTIVITIES

- Children play charades to depict different emotions.

- Children use different facial features to act out different emotions.

- Class compile a mind map of emotion faces and emotion words.

- Children listen to different songs and connect an emotion with that song.

- Children create an emotion word crossword.

- Children take pictures of one another 'posing' different emotion faces.

6.3 Empty Emotions

Unjumble the words below to find words that match emotions, then draw the emotions in the face and match the words.

Describe a scene when you felt the emotion – what were you thinking at the time you were feeling this way? Record this scene by writing about it or painting it.

AMD

Emotion

....

A time when

....

My thinking was

....

CREADS

Emotion

....

A time when

....

My thinking was

....

VERBA

Emotion

....

A time when

....

My thinking was

....

MALC

Emotion

....

A time when

....

My thinking was

....

ASD

Emotion

....

A time when

....

My thinking was

....

PAPHY

Emotion

....

A time when

....

My thinking was

....

ROWIRED

Emotion

....

A time when

....

My thinking was

....

RUDOP

Emotion

....

A time when

....

My thinking was

....

6.4 Dear Diary – teacher notes

ACTIVITY OBJECTIVES

- Children reflect on their day via a feelings filter, the daily Dear Dairy.
- Children use their Dear Diary to debrief their day.
- Children begin to associate feelings with different social events experienced by them throughout the day.

WORKSHEET REQUIREMENTS

You will need:

- Notebook
- Pen/pencil
- Stapler or scissors and glue

My feelings are up in the air

MAIN ACTIVITY

- Children compile a Dear Diary booklet using the template on the worksheet.
- Children listen to their peers sharing different Dear Diary entries.
- Children predict what might happen if/when different emotions are experienced for the same event.

EXTENSION ACTIVITIES

- Children make individual daily diary sequence ladders, commencing with daily events at the beginning of the day (e.g. waking up, getting dressed, then eating breakfast). They record the events next to the emotions they associate with them.
- Children teach the Dear Diary strategy to younger children.
- Children work in groups to think about and tally the similarities and differences between their daily events and associated emotions.

6.4 Dear Diary

Sometimes we may be confused about what to do when we have a certain feeling. If we are feeling confused, we may talk to someone or write down our thoughts, and this may help with working out our confusion.

My feelings are up in the air

Below we have provided a Dear Diary page. Make a booklet using this template for times when you need to sort out your feelings. You can either staples the pages together or glue them into a notebook/exercise book.

Date: ____/____/____

Dear Diary

Today I'm feeling (circle the feeling)

HAPPY   EXCITED   SAD   CONFUSED   TIRED

FRIGHTENED   RELAXED   LONELY   TENSE   ANGRY

Because . . . .

. . . .

If I'm feeling...

SAD or ANGRY – I can cheer up by thinking of something or someone I really like

CONFUSED or FRIGHTENED – I can talk to someone or write in this diary

LONELY – I can telephone, email or visit a friend when I go home

TIRED – I can rest with my head on my desk or have a nap if I'm at home

TENSE – I can do some of my de-stress muscle activities

HAPPY – I can keep feeling that way and share that feeling with others

EXCITED – I can smile and share my news

RELAXED – I can feel peaceful

6.5 Extended Emotions – teacher notes

ACTIVITY OBJECTIVES

- Children are introduced to an extreme emotions scale.
- Children complete a personal catastrophe feeling scale.
- Children learn more degrees of emotions.
- Children learn that different feelings can be associated with the same events.

WORKSHEET REQUIREMENTS

You will need:

- A4 paper
- Pen/pencil

MAIN ACTIVITY

- Children use this worksheet as a reality check at school/home.
- Children assign different numerical values to different feelings. They discuss the similarities and differences in the values and scales of individual children.

EXTENSION ACTIVITIES

- Children can take photographs of school and home situations that represent events on the scale.
- Helper introduces the concept of the national emergency telephone number – if the situation is an emergency then it equates with phoning that emergency number.
- Children think about helpful ideas for what to do at different levels on their scale.
- Children compare and contrast their scales, and discuss any differences

6.5 Extended Emotions

We feel different emotions at different times during different occasions.

Let's see if you can work out what emotions you would feel/have felt during the following times. Have a look at the emotions scale from 1 to 6 and write the emotion number in the boxes below to match with the event. Discuss with your class/group/helper.

1	2	3	4	5	6
HAPPINESS	SURPRISE	WORRY	SADNESS	ANNOYANCE	ANGER

	Someone teases me.
	I witness a friend being teased.
	It's my birthday.
	Some children in my class won't let me play their game.
	It's my turn for morning talk.
	I am in a walkathon.
	I am sick and have to stay away from school.
	My friends ask me to play a game with them.
	I hurt my head.
	I have a fight with my friends.
	We are going on a family holiday.
	Other:

6.6 Merry Medals – teacher notes

ACTIVITY OBJECTIVES

- Children develop awareness about the significance of feeling happy within themselves and being proud of who they are.
- Children's self-identity is promoted and nurtured.
- Children are aware of when they are happy.

WORKSHEET REQUIREMENTS

You will need:

- A4 paper
- Pen/pencil
- Scissors
- Hole punch
- Ribbon

MAIN ACTIVITY

- Children talk with their helper about a time during the day when they were happy.
- Children use the worksheet activity to think about what makes them happy and how they respond when feeling happy.
- Children can wear the medals they produce from the worksheet as reminders of happy times.

EXTENSION ACTIVITIES

- Children tally the number of times they recorded themselves being happy and the number of times they recorded others being happy (specific peers or whole class). Children graph these times individually and as a class.
- Helper photographs the children 'in the act' of being happy.
- Children create a class 'Being Happy' jingle.
- Children write a newspaper advertisement about the gift of happiness/being happy.
- Children design a project about the feeling 'happy': they could think about the emotion 'happy' and write about/draw people, events or images that give them that happy feeling, or they could cut out scenes or words from magazines that equate with their understanding of 'happy'.

6.6 Merry Medals

Happiness is a positive feeling that helps you feel good inside, and it shows on the outside. Let's explore the HAPPINESS feeling. Think before writing your experiences about being HAPPY – what you feel in your heart, what you think in your head and how your body responds.

Share your thoughts with your helper before writing them down on the medals.

Cut out your medals and use a hole punch to make a hole for you to thread your ribbon through. Then wear your medals with pride!

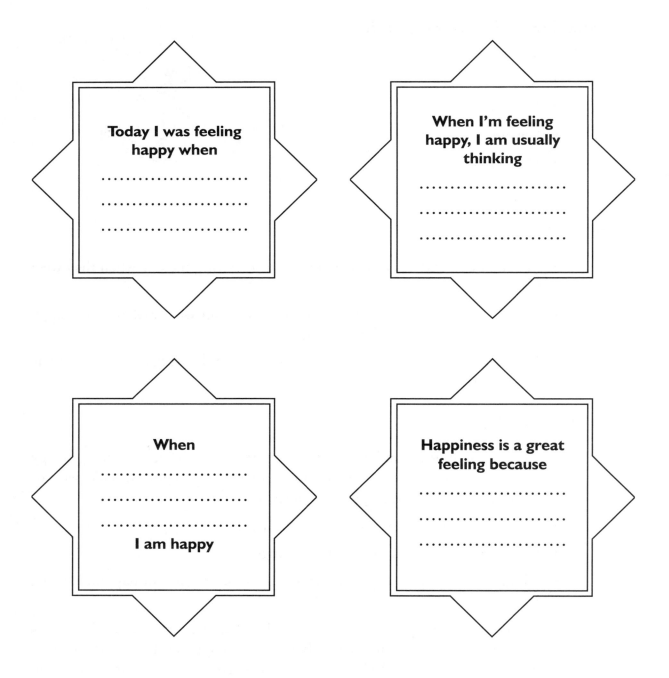

Today I was feeling happy when

....

....

....

When I'm feeling happy, I am usually thinking

....

....

....

When

....

....

....

I am happy

Happiness is a great feeling because

....

....

....

7
Attaining Independence – Literacy Themed

Importance of the capability

Children who learn to think for themselves are more likely to act independently. They are more willing to try new things, are self-directing and take responsibility for tasks to be completed. Children develop independence as they self-manage learning, interact with others and make judgements about events, activities and choices.

When faced with jobs/tasks/challenges, children who are independent (1) think wisely as to how to go about achieving them and (2) apply themselves and 'go for it', that is, they have a go, ask for help and try a different approach if their initial attempt is unsuccessful. They have an 'I can do it' rather than 'I can't and won't do it' attitude. They are prepared to give things a go, willing to seek support when they need it and persist with the task at hand.

List of activities

7.1 Doom or Do   –   Situation steps

7.2 Healthy Hygiene   –   Frequency counter

7.3 Exciting Event   –   Event planner

7.4 Easy Exercise   –   Exercise programme

7.5 Me Mobile   –   Independence statements

7.6 Crack the Code   –   Word search

7.1 Doom or Do – teacher notes

ACTIVITY OBJECTIVES

- Children learn the connection between cause and effect – giving up or keeping going.

- Children learn more about the potential impact of helpful and unhelpful choices – DOOM versus DO choices.

- Children learn more about taking responsibility for their choices.

- Children think about alternative solutions to social events.

WORKSHEET REQUIREMENTS

You will need:

- A4 paper

- Pen/pencil

MAIN ACTIVITY

- Children use the worksheet to think about DO and DOOM choices.

- Children replay their day – making DOOM choices and talking about likely outcomes versus making DO choices and talking about possible outcomes.

- Children record their DO and DOOM decisions for a specific time period, using the chart on the worksheet.

EXTENSION ACTIVITIES

- Children make distinctions between the DO and DOOM choices of planting seeds/plants in different parts of the garden.

- Children make up and perform a song about DO rather than DOOM choices.

7.1 Doom or Do

When something happens that spoils your day, you can feel defeated, give up and blame other people. We have the power to change this thinking and feeling by making wiser choices. You can either ask for help and try something different OR give up and complain.

We have given you some examples of DOOM and DO scenarios. Discuss them with your helper and then write/illustrate some of your own examples of times when you thought it was a DOOM situation, and the choices you made/could have made to move toward a DO situation.

SITUATION	DOOM	DO
No hat to play outside	Don't worry about it and run around in the sun.	Play undercover and remember to pack hat every day.
Remembered the library bag but forgot the library book	Tell teacher you don't feel well at reading time.	Choose another book and put it on hold, and pack book on the next library day.
Forgot to bring lunch to school	Share your friends' lunch.	Tell teacher and try to remember to check morning timetable before leaving home in the future.
Left project at home on the due day	Tell teacher the dog ate your work.	Talk to teacher and remember to check diary for due dates.

7.2 Healthy Hygiene – teacher notes

ACTIVITY OBJECTIVES

- Children discuss the concept of personal hygiene.

- Children take more responsibility for being more independent with personal hygiene – learning exactly what to do to stay healthy.

- Children learn more about the implications of remembering/neglecting personal hygiene.

WORKSHEET REQUIREMENTS

You will need:

- A4 paper

- Pen/pencil

MAIN ACTIVITY

- Children use the worksheet activity to record the frequency of their personal hygiene habits and tasks.

- Children look at their results, discuss with their helper, and evaluate whether they need to change their habits.

EXTENSION ACTIVITIES

- Children make up a class quiz about personal hygiene.

- Children create personal hygiene cartoons for younger children.

- Children record the hygiene habits of a pet at home or school.

- Children give hands-on demonstrations of why, how, where and when to perform personal hygiene tasks.

- Children interview different generations in their family and record their hygiene habits.

- Children research and do a self-paced project on the invention of toothpaste, soap or the comb.

- Children do a craft activity with recycled hygiene material (e.g. old toothbrush, nailbrush).

7.2 Healthy Hygiene

It's very important to be hygienic in order to have a healthy body. As you get older you become more independent with your hygiene but you are still learning about frequency. Below is a frequency hygiene table with a frequency scale you use to complete the table. Everyone's hygiene habits are different, and you may like to add more things that are not mentioned here. You may like to share your table with your helper if you want further advice on how frequent you should make your habits. Discuss what frequency would be healthy for each hygiene habit.

Frequency scale

1. Twice daily
2. Daily
3. Twice weekly

4. Weekly
5. Monthly
6. Yearly
7. Never

Frequency	Hygiene
	Wash body with soap
	Shampoo hair
	Wash hands after toilet
	Put on deodorant
	Brush teeth
	Floss teeth
	Brush/comb hair
	Wear clean uniform/clothing
	Trim nails
	Visit dentist
	Change underwear

7.3 Exciting Event – teacher notes

ACTIVITY OBJECTIVES

- Children develop familiarity with the sequence involved in independently planning different events.

- Children take more responsibility for seeing an event through from beginning to end.

- Children learn the importance of behind the scenes organisation when planning an event on their own.

WORKSHEET REQUIREMENTS

You will need:

- A4 paper

- Pen/pencil

MAIN ACTIVITY

- Children use the worksheet as an introduction to breaking an organisational task into logical steps. Using their findings, they can then progress to the following activities:

  - Children rank their event preparation tasks in order of importance.

  - Children time each segment involved in planning their event.

  - Children hypothesise and compare the organisation required for their scheduled events.

  - Children plan weekly events for home and class.

EXTENSION ACTIVITIES

- Helper jumbles up the sequence of planning for an event and asks children to rearrange in the correct sequence. Remember, it is important to know numbers so that games can be planned. For example, if there will be two people you'll need a two-player game, but if there will be five then you'll need a game for five. You'll need to know who's coming to know how much food is required. If, for example, someone is coeliac, you'll need to know this to plan the menu accordingly.

- Children use recycled material to design a poster promoting their planned event.

7.3 Exciting Event

event

Because you are now an organised person, you can plan for events such as birthday parties, play dates, a shopping trip, etc.

Most events need some sort of planning, for example who to invite, what food to have, written invitations so your event can run smoothly.

Below we have provided you with simple steps to arrange a birthday party and a play date.

Discuss these steps with your helper, and then write your own steps to plan for your own event, whether it be real or pretend.

Birthday Party			
Write and send invites	Plan menu	Plan games and decorations	Birthday party!

Play Date			
Invite friend	Plan play time	Prepare food	Play date!

7.4 Easy Exercise – teacher notes

ACTIVITY OBJECTIVES

- Children learn about the importance of regular exercise.
- Children follow through with their nominated exercise plan as per the exercise programme schedule.
- Children become a little more familiar with the types of exercise that promote strength, flexibility and endurance.

WORKSHEET REQUIREMENTS

You will need:

- A4 coloured paper
- Pen
- Scissors
- Laminating device
- Hanging device
- Non-permanent marker

MAIN ACTIVITY

- Children use the worksheet to create an exercise schedule and complete their nominated schedule for the week.
- Children evaluate and record on a graph the improvement in their fitness level for each exercise each day.
- Children journal about the difference/lack of difference exercising makes to their physical and mental well-being.
- Children research the life story of a famous sports person in a relatively unknown or unrecognised sport.

EXTENSION ACTIVITIES

- Children develop an imaginary exercise programme for an alien.
- Children record their personal best for their daily exercise programme.
- Children actively exercise with a family member.
- Children design an obstacle course with recycled material.

7.4 Easy Exercise

It is important for your health that you do some physical exercise. Talk to your helper about the types of exercise you do and write them down in the gaps below.

Work out how much time you need to spend exercising each week to keep you healthy and fit for your age and build (everyone's time may be different). Then enlarge the planner onto A4 coloured paper, laminate it and hang it in your room/class to remind you to exercise. You can use a non-permanent market to monitor each week's exercise plan.

Types of exercises I can do:

....

....

....

....

Day	Activity	Time
Monday		
Tuesday		
Wednesday		
Thursday		
Friday		
Saturday		
Sunday		
Total time		

7.5 Me Mobile – teacher notes

ACTIVITY OBJECTIVES

- Children's awareness and appreciation of their uniqueness is raised.
- Children acknowledge what they can do independently at different stages of their life – baby, toddler, nursery, pre-school, Year 1, etc.
- Children appreciate the same and different aspect of themselves, peers and family members.

WORKSHEET REQUIREMENTS

You will need:

- A4 coloured paper
- Scissors
- Colouring crayons, pencils, etc.
- Hole puncher
- String
- Glue and glitter
- Coat hanger

MAIN ACTIVITY

- Children use the Me Mobile worksheet to highlight their own gifts.
- Children turn their work into a mobile which will function as a visual reminder of their achievements.

EXTENSION ACTIVITIES

- Children highlight one another's gifts through poetry/music.
- Children collect 'ME' data from each classmate to compile a class talents chart.
- On a regular basis helper invites children to identify what they appreciate about their classmates and teaching staff.
- Children compile a 'ME' resume.
- Children interview an older person in their family and talk to them about which of their traits they see in their younger relatives.
- Children identify and celebrate the talents of different family members.
- Children create a 'ME' milestone road to record personal milestones and achievements, such as losing their first teeth, starting school and joining the scouts.
- Children design a 'ME' placemat for each family member.

7.5 Me Mobile

When you can do things by yourself, you are 'independent'. Discuss with your helper the things that you are 'independent' with.

Then fill in the boxes below with your answers. Cut out the boxes and make and decorate a 'ME' mobile so you can be reminded about the things that you don't need help with any more.

At school I can **by myself**	**At home I can** **by myself**
With my special interest I can **by myself**	**At a restaurant I can** **by myself**

7.6 Crack the Code – teacher notes

ACTIVITY OBJECTIVES

- Children discuss the attributes of independence.

- Children name which of these strengths and attributes they have already achieved and which are yet to be mastered.

WORKSHEET REQUIREMENTS

You will need:

- A4 paper

- Dictionary

- Pen/pencil

MAIN ACTIVITY

- Children use the worksheet activity and a dictionary to familiarise themselves with vocabulary relating to independence.

- Children select different attributes of independence and write a story about them.

- Children draw pictures of themselves which can be joined together to make a 'ME' paper patchwork quilt.

- Children design symbols to represent each of the independence attributes, such as a lion for courage or a leopard for being energetic.

EXTENSION ACTIVITIES

- Children play charades to act out the independence attributes.

- Children design and construct a woven totem pole of 'ME' attributes using cardboard, pencils, craft materials, etc.

- Children create a personal independence attribute talking stick. The talking stick represents a microphone, and can be a creative piece of art made from lots of different things.

7.6 Crack the Code

Here is a word puzzle for you to crack. Find the 11 words listed inside the puzzle. The words can go any direction: north, south, east, west, or diagonally.

Look up the words in a dictionary, write down their definitions and see what they all have in common.

ATTITUDE	CAPABLE	CHALLENGE
CONFIDENCE	DETERMINED	EFFORT
INDEPENDENCE	MYSELF	PRACTICE
RESPONSIBLE	SUCCESS	

E	D	U	T	I	T	T	A	Z	L	V	E	C	S	K
M	Y	S	E	L	F	T	Z	Z	B	C	T	O	S	E
F	Z	I	R	K	Y	D	I	E	N	H	I	N	E	P
B	W	E	N	L	S	V	G	E	H	K	O	F	C	Z
O	C	W	X	M	S	H	D	I	M	D	A	I	C	K
D	R	E	S	P	O	N	S	I	B	L	E	D	U	U
A	E	D	S	B	E	S	E	C	V	L	M	E	S	J
G	C	T	P	P	M	C	H	F	B	S	L	N	J	D
E	A	C	E	X	G	A	I	A	F	Y	F	C	C	J
X	N	D	W	R	L	G	P	T	Y	O	Q	E	V	J
P	N	X	S	L	M	A	A	D	C	G	R	F	H	E
I	N	H	E	Q	C	I	Q	A	Q	A	J	T	N	G
G	P	N	P	Y	Q	K	N	T	H	S	R	E	U	L
M	G	G	S	L	P	X	V	E	Y	M	J	P	O	U
E	H	G	A	G	Q	G	G	A	D	A	Z	O	D	B

8 Communicating Effectively – Technology Themed

Importance of the capability

Children communicate using gestures, sounds and language, both verbally and non-verbally. They listen to, engage with and interpret ideas and opinions as they communicate with others. Learning to communicate effectively is about stating clearly what you are thinking and feeling in a calm and confident way. Good communication is positive, respectful and appropriate.

Effective communicators engage children in discussions to help them learn social skills. They provide literacy-enriched environments, modelling written and oral language, and encouraging children to express themselves through language.

Adults encourage children to become effective communicators when they use 'I' messages. 'You' messages often use blaming words and attack others; for example, 'You shouldn't say that!' as opposed to 'I don't like what you are saying.' 'I' messages focus attention on the speaker rather than the listener, enabling the speaker to express situations/problems/issues in a respectful and assertive manner. People who say 'I' take responsibility for their actions.

List of activities

8.1 Self Study   –   Personal record
8.2 Regular Reporting   –   Communication
8.3 Respectful Responses – Oral responses
8.4 Text Talk   –   Contact conversation
8.5 Solution Steps   –   Social problem solving
8.6 Jargon Jumble   –   Social play sequencing

8.1 Self Study – teacher notes

ACTIVITY OBJECTIVES

- Children interact verbally with others about what they enjoy and what they find frustrating/difficult/challenging – their likes and dislikes about home and family living.

- Children engage in enjoyable interaction with others about their likes and dislikes – highs and lows.

- Children express themselves verbally and non-verbally.

WORKSHEET REQUIREMENTS

You will need:

- A4 paper

- Pen/pencil

MAIN ACTIVITY

- Children work individually completing the questionnaire on the worksheet before sharing their responses with peers.

- Children work in small groups of three or four designing logos promoting their school/family. They present logos to their class and ask for suggestions about how to improve them, then paste them on the class blog/school website/ school newsletter.

EXTENSION ACTIVITIES

- Children ask each other to identify similarities and differences in their questionnaire responses.

- Children compile a tally of questionnaire responses about school and family.

- Children interview family members and record their highs and lows, their likes and dislikes. They choose school as one area and holidays as the second area.

8.1 Self Study

I like this song

We all have opinions about what we like and what we dislike, what the high and the low spots are in our days, what we enjoy and what we find frustrating, difficult or challenging. We are not the same in how we view the world, so our likes and dislikes will not be the same for everyone.

When we communicate with other people about our highs and lows, our likes and dislikes, others get to know us a little better.

On the next few pages, write about and then chat about what you enjoy and what you find frustrating – what you like and what you dislike. We have chosen the focus to be school and family. Think carefully about your responses to each question. Share your ideas – first by answering the questions and second by discussing your answers with your helper/peers.

My School

I enjoy...
Three things I really enjoy about my school are:

....

....

....

One of my favourite things to do in my 'free/spare' time at school is:

....

The best thing about my school is:

....

I would recommend my school as a great school because:

....

I find difficult...
Three things I find difficult/frustrating about my school are:

....

....

....

One thing that really annoys me at school is:

....

The worst thing about my school is:

....

My Family

I enjoy...
Three things I really like about my family are:

....

....

....

One of my favourite things to do in my 'free/spare' time with my family is:

....

The best thing about my family is:

....

I would recommend my family as a great family because:

....

I find frustrating...
Three things I find frustrating about my family are:

....

....

....

One thing that really annoys me about my family is:

....

The worse thing about my family is:

....

8.2 Regular Reporting – teacher notes

ACTIVITY OBJECTIVES

- Children communicate personal ideas and opinions about their week of learning.

- Children deepen their understanding and appreciation of how communication by regular reporting works.

- Children interact verbally and non-verbally with others about their week of learning.

- Children learn that their voice is heard through the Regular Reporting proforma.

WORKSHEET REQUIREMENTS

You will need:

- A4 paper

- Pen/pencil

MAIN ACTIVITY

- Children use the proforma on the worksheet to express their ideas on how they've been learning that week.

- Parents, teachers and other helpers are also invited to let children know their thoughts on what they have achieved and what can be improved upon.

- Each week children record the highlight of their learning/progress during the week and this is displayed on a board in the classroom or on the fridge door at home.

EXTENSION ACTIVITIES

- Helper interviews children about their special achievements/memorable moments during the week. This is converted into a class PowerPoint and showcased at the next parent-teacher evening.

- Children use different texts to communicate their weekly learning.

- Children keep a journal in cartoon form of their weekly learning/memorable moments.

- The class make a video of their weekly learning and post it on the school blog/website.

8.2 Regular Reporting

Communication is crucial for exchanging ideas, questions, feelings and thoughts. A regular report where everyone communicates about the same topic ensures everybody stays on the same page and remains in the loop.

Fill out the proforma below at the end of every week or month. Use your section, 'Me – Student', to let everyone else know how you feel and what you think about how you got on that week. Then your parent, teacher, teacher's assistant, schoolofficer and any other helpers can give you their comments on things you've done well and areas for improvement.

Regular Reporting week/month ending   /   /
Student Name .... Class ....
Me – Student
My parent
My teacher
Teacher's assistant/Schoolofficer
Other

8.3 Respectful Responses – teacher notes

ACTIVITY OBJECTIVES

- Children think about alternative/constructive responses to put downs.

- Children communicate with others in ways that build up relationships.

- Children discuss the difference between boosters (compliments) and put downs.

WORKSHEET REQUIREMENTS

You will need:

- A4 paper

- Pen/pencil

- Video recorder (optional)

MAIN ACTIVITY

- Children begin by using the worksheet to explore respectful and disrespectful responses.

- Children think of respectful (friendly) and disrespectful (unfriendly) ways of saying the same message and record these responses on video.

- Children play charades, communicating the verbal message in a non-verbal way.

- Children compare and contrast non-verbal messages connected with responses that are helpful and unhelpful/friendly and unfriendly.

EXTENSION ACTIVITIES

- Children make up a positive words/phrase jingle. Once the jingle is composed, they perform it for an audience.

- Children design a snakes and ladders game with booster and put down phrases and make up the rules (e.g. when you pick up a put down card you go down the snake and when you pick up a booster card you go up the ladder).

- Children make a list of positive phrases from around the world in different languages (e.g. French, Spanish, etc.).

8.3 Respectful Responses

If you want to be a friend and to have friends you need to learn how to communicate effectively. One very important way of doing this is making sure you speak to your friend with kind words (e.g. 'Can we play together?', 'I like it when you make that face,' etc.).

When something happens, children can choose to respond verbally and/or non-verbally in ways that are polite/friendly or impolite/unfriendly. The best way of communicating with others is the polite and friendly way, although this is easier said than done at times!

It is important for children to connect and to be friends with others. Children need to learn polite and friendly ways of communicating with others – they need to learn the language of kind words.

Practise with writing alternative (KIND) responses to the put down. Share your responses.

ACTION	PUT DOWN	KIND WORDS
Pestering	You stink	1. Please can you leave me on my own, thank you 2. 3.
Joining in a game	No, because you are stupid	1. You can join in the next game 2. 3.
Pushing in		1. 2. 3.
Cheating		1. 2. 3.
Gossiping		1. 2. 3.
Other		1. 2. 3.

8.4 Text Talk – teacher notes

ACTIVITY OBJECTIVES

- Children broaden their communication repertoire of what to say when talking with others.

- Children learn more about respectful ways of talking with others.

- Children think about the importance of communicating well with others.

WORKSHEET REQUIREMENTS

You will need:

- A4 paper

- Pen/pencil

MAIN ACTIVITY

- Children use the worksheet to gather ideas and discuss the etiquette of texting.

- Children talk about different communication media, such as talking face to face and texting. They debate the pros and cons of a texting society.

EXTENSION ACTIVITIES

- Children work in pairs designing a poster promoting safe texting for audiences of different generations, e.g. children in nursery and pre-school, primary school, middle school; grandparents; children for whom English is a second language; children on a school trip.

- Children work together in a small group of three or four and create a huge collage science fiction mobile phone for texting in another galaxy.

- Children work in a small group compiling a texting list (e.g. please = pls).

8.4 Text Talk

Children use a range of texts when communicating with others, including texting via a mobile phone.

Below we have provided you with different texting scenarios. Think how you would respond to each situation. Would your response be the same if you were texting or talking face to face? Practise what you would text in each of these situations.

- Match the scenario letters (A, B, C, etc.) with the person you would call (e.g. parent/carer, older family member, etc.). You can add other names if you need to.

- Write a text response message.

- Discuss your responses with your helper/class.

	Texting scenario
A	You forgot who is collecting you from school
B	You are researching a family history project and want to get information from the oldest member of your extended family
C	It is your aunt's/uncle's birthday
D	A relative sent you a birthday card
E	You forgot what your homework was
F	You are planning a sleepover
G	You need to confirm your ride to Taekwondo with your buddy
H	You accidentally left your bag on the train
I	You want to see the latest movie at the cinema

1	2	3
4	**5**	**6**
7	**8**	**9**

1. MUM OR FEMALE CARER	2. RELATIVE
3. FRIEND	4. TAEKWONDO BUDDY
5. GRANDPARENT	6. DAD OR MALE CARER
7. AUNT/UNCLE	8. TRAIN LOST PROPERTY
9. SCHOOL PEER	

8.5 Solution Steps – teacher notes

ACTIVITY OBJECTIVES

- Children learn about and apply a social problem solving sequence to a particular social scenario.

- Children think about possible solutions to different social scenarios.

WORKSHEET REQUIREMENTS

You will need:

- A4 paper

- Pen/pencil or crayons

MAIN ACTIVITY

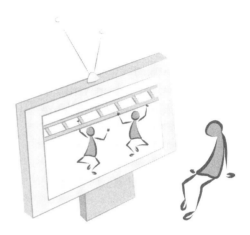

- Children complete the worksheet and compare and contrast their sequence solutions. They discuss the similarities and differences, and identify and discuss which sequences would be more successful and why. Helper suggests alternatives to those whose success rate is low.

EXTENSION ACTIVITIES

- Children follow the problem solving sequence to work out the following conflicts: children wanting to play but not pack away; children pushing others so they can be first in the line; and children refusing to let others join in the play.

- Children work in small groups of two or three compiling a problem solving sequence for keeping our planet clean, for example, recycling rubbish.

- To demonstrate other ways of communicating, children use sign language to communicate different social play sequences. They will first need to research the American Sign Language (ASL) dictionary so that they can fingerspell their message.

8.5 Solution Steps

Sometimes we communicate with others in negative and unhelpful ways. You need to learn positive ways of communicating. First you need to become calm in body and mind so that you can work out what the problem is, then you need to work out what the possible solutions to the problem are. Next decide what are your preferred solutions. Then follow through with them.

Complete the social problem solving sequence below, beginning at number 1, for a time when you could have used these steps. Share your thinking with peers and/or adult helper.

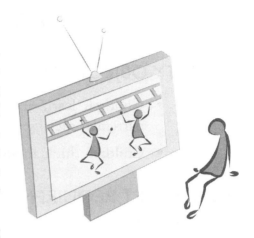

5. DOING IT

4. CHOOSING BEST SOLUTION/S

3. THINKING ABOUT SOLUTION/S

2. NAMING PROBLEM

1. CALMING DOWN

DRAW YOUR SOLUTION HERE

8.6 Jargon Jumble – teacher notes

ACTIVITY OBJECTIVES

- Children work out wise ways of communicating when they are involved/wanting to be involved in social situations.

- Children problem solve the steps involved in social situations and then sequence them in order from beginning to end.

- Children put different cycles of events into a sequence.

WORKSHEET REQUIREMENTS

You will need:

- A4 paper

- Pen/pencil

Solutions are given on p.160.

MAIN ACTIVITY

- Children complete the worksheet and then role-play each step in the social sequence.

- Children then use mime to communicate the same information in each social situation.

EXTENSION ACTIVITIES

- Children make up a social sequence storybook taking photographs of one another as they follow the social sequence for specific social skills.

- Children work together in a small group of three or four researching ants in nature, in particular the cooperation of an ant colony as they take turns.

8.6 Jargon Jumble

Learning smart ways of communicating effectively when you want to join in a game, listen, wait your turn or cooperate is very important.

Unjumble the words in the sentences and number the steps in each sequence to uncover friendly ways of communicating in different social situations.

Next level...

JOINING IN

TIME WAIT THE RIGHT FOR

SAY, 'JOIN I CAN IN' OR 'PLAY CAN TOO I'

ASKING A BIG TAKE BEFORE JOIN IN TO BREATH

JOIN IN TO STOP, RIGHT THINK THIS IS IF LOOK AROUND AND THE TIME

LISTENING

DO ASKED OR GET REPLY, AS MORE INFORMATION

SAID ABOUT BEING WHAT IS THINK

QUIET STILL, AND CALM STAY

LOOK IN THE DIRECTION OF STOP, THE SPEAKER AND THINK

WAITING MY TURN

QUIETLY TAKE BREATHS AND SOME WAIT DEEP

HAVE THE TURN AND WAIT FOR YOUR TIME RIGHT

I CAN WAIT, TO STOP AND DO IT, THINK BUT IT'S HARD

COOPERATING

YOUR SHARE IDEAS

OTHERS' LISTEN TO IDEAS

IF NECESSARY MORE INFORMATION GET

THE DIRECTIONS TO THINK STOP, AND LISTEN

---

9 Relaxing and Energising – Cooking Themed

Importance of the capability

Relaxing and energising is about letting go of lifestyles, tension and worry that are creating a strain on your body – mentally and physically. Relaxation can…

- reduce anxiety and help you to conserve energy

- increase your self-control when dealing with stress

- help you recognise the difference between tense muscles and relaxed ones

- help you physically and emotionally handle daily demands
- help you remain alert, energetic and productive.

The overall purpose of relaxing and energising is to give children an awareness of their muscle tension. When children learn to become aware of this tension, they will be aware of how to control it by learning how to relax so that their body feels calmer. The benefits of relaxing and energising include lowered blood pressure, reduced anxiety, lower oxygen consumption and improved concentration. Children develop a sense of being in control of themselves, which contributes to them developing self-confidence and self-esteem.

Relaxation and energising can help children put things in perspective. Children learn to change pace, to become still, and therefore are more open to learning new information, are more creative and use their imagination and problem-solving skills.

List of activities

9.1 Food Fantasy   –   Visualisation
9.2 Relaxation Remedies   –   Acrostic poem
9.3 Laugh Loudly   –   Laugh-a-thon
9.4 Balanced Breath   –   Breathing techniques
9.5 Kitchen Kicks   –   Energising exercises
9.6 Sleep Strategies   –   Differentiation tables

9.1 Food Fantasy – teacher notes

ACTIVITY OBJECTIVES

- Children work with visualisation as a self-calming stress reduction strategy.

- Children develop some more familiarity with visualisation as a way to slow their body, thus experiencing a sense of peace and calm.

- Children begin to see the cause–effect connection between visualising themselves self-calming and being able to de-stress themselves.

WORKSHEET REQUIREMENTS

You will need:

- A4 paper

- Pen/pencil, colouring crayons

MAIN ACTIVITY

- Helper schedules a time each day when children can engage in this visualisation – after break/before bed.

- Helper has a visualisation script available in the sacred space of the classroom/ home for children to access when the need arises.

- Helper records familiar adults (e.g. parents) reading the visualisation script on the worksheet and plays it back to the children.

EXTENSION ACTIVITIES

- Helper introduces progressive muscle relaxation and combines this with visualisation.

- Children draw/paint images from their visualisations over a period of time and use them to create a personalised mobile.

9.1 Food Fantasy

It is important to relax and let go of worries and tensions.

Here we use visualisation, where you can sit or lay on the floor with your eyes shut, and relax as your helper reads the script. Imagine you are a chef cooking a lovely meal; this will help divert your thoughts from worries and enable you to relax.

Afterwards, draw a picture about your visualisation and share it with your helper and/or peers.

Food fantasy visualisation script

You are a chef about to embark on a cooking challenge. To participate in this competition you must first reach a completely relaxed state so your body can fit into the specially designed apron. You are standing in the doorway of the kitchen.

Close your eyes. To reach this super-relaxed state you must focus on your breathing. Don't change your breathing, but just listen to your breath and breathe in and out as your would normally do. As you breathe out say to yourself the word 'relax'. Breathe in; breathe out saying the word 'relax' to yourself. (Allow a minute of silence.)

You are now ready to be fitted into your apron. Your helper helps you with your apron. Once fitted into your apron and with your chef hat on, your helper leaves the kitchen through the swinging doors. You are alone in the kitchen. You can hear a bubbling noise as a pot of water boils on the stove. Now we will commence a countdown from 10 to 1. When we reach the number 1 you will be in a super-relaxed state in your apron and will be ready to cook.

10   You feel your whole body start to melt

9   You feel your body sinking

8   You feel your eyes, mouth and face relax

7   You feel your neck muscles relax

6   You feel your arms become heavy

5   You feel your stomach relax

4   You feel your legs turn to jelly

3   You feel your feet relax

2   You are in a completely relaxed state

1   You are in a super relaxed and calm state

Your body is limp and is like jelly. Now your body is a perfect fit to your apron and you are ready to cook. A bench appears with all the ingredients you need to cook and prepare your favourite dish. It is a quick dish, but something very yummy. I will leave you for a few minutes to have some fun, and when it's time to finish cooking I will call you.

(After a few minutes) Now it is time to finish. Have a last look around. You remove your chef's hat. Your helper assists you to remove your apron.

Open your eyes wriggle your fingers and toes. Welcome back!

9.2 Relaxation Remedies – teacher notes

ACTIVITY OBJECTIVES

- Children broaden their definition of the term 'relax' to include both active and quiet activities.
- Children discuss the importance of having a relaxed body and a relaxed mind.

WORKSHEET REQUIREMENTS

You will need:

- Recycled material such as greeting cards, old puzzle pieces
- A4 paper
- Pens/crayons
- Scissors
- Glue
- Dictionary

MAIN ACTIVITY

- Children follow the instructions on the worksheet to mind map ideas about relaxation. They can use the word 'relax' as the focal point.
- Children discuss active ways of relaxing and compare with quiet ways of relaxing.
- Children discuss the importance of having a relaxed body and a relaxed mind.
- Children debate the value of exciting and slowing down the body as a form of relaxation.
- Children present an acrostic poem explaining the word 'relax'.

EXTENSION ACTIVITIES

- Children formulate a group relaxation ideas plan – on-the-spot and short-term and long-term ideas (e.g. breathing in and out, skipping, going for a daily bike ride).
- Children research how children living elsewhere in the world relax at school and home.
- Children create a magazine mosaic, using recycled magazines, of the word 'relax'.

9.2 Relaxation Remedies

When we are relaxing we might lie down and read a book, go for a run, listen to music or go for a bike ride. Some of the things we do keep our body active and some slow it down. Think about what happens to our heartbeat and our breathing when we are active and when we slow down. Did you know that being active quickens our heart rate and resting slows it down? Both forms of activity can be relaxing. Mind map reasons why this might be the case.

There are many words that relate to the meaning RELAX.

Below we have provided you with a list of some of these words. Check your understanding of these words by looking them up in a dictionary. See if your understanding and the dictionary's definition match. Draw your preferred definition for each word.

Then write an acrostic poem using some of the words from your list. Decorate the border of your page with recycled material, such as greeting cards. Share your poem and your page with your friends and family.

REST

REFRESH

RESPITE

_____

EASE

ENERGY

ENJOY

_____

LAZE

LAUGH

LEISURE

_____

ART

ATTITUDE

AMUSEMENT

_____

EXHILIRATING

EXERCISE

EXHALE

✓

R

E

L

A

X

9.3 Laugh Loudly – teacher notes

ACTIVITY OBJECTIVES

- Children learn more about the significance of laughter in mental well-being.
- Children investigate the importance of laughter in mental well-being – for themselves, classmates and families.
- Children think about and plan for bringing laughter into their daily life.

WORKSHEET REQUIREMENTS

You will need:

- A4 paper
- Pen/pencil

MAIN ACTIVITY

- Children use the worksheet activity to start thinking about how laughter makes them feel.
- Children research the value and significance of daily laughter for themselves, peers and family members. Helper discusses with children what they have learned from their research. Children record their findings in a book about 'Laughter'.
- Working in pairs, children write funny lyrics to school chants.
- Children or helpers photograph people laughing and the children use the photographs to create a 'Catch others in the act of laughing' class/school and family notice board.

EXTENSION ACTIVITIES

- Children research and do a group presentation on Patch Adams.
- Children think and chat about living with no laugher. They create two villages – in village 1 laughter is not allowed; in village 2 laughter is encouraged. Children look for differences between the village people.
- Children use crepe paper to make animal facemasks – happy, smiling, laughing masks compared with grumpy, frowning, snarling masks.

9.3 Laugh Loudly

It is healthy to laugh. Laughter releases endorphins, chemicals in your brain that give you a feeling of well-being. Laughter helps reduce stress and increases calmness in your mind and your body.

There are lots of things you can do to have laughter in your day: watching funny TV shows, reading funny stories, telling funny jokes, listening to funny jokes.

Think about what makes you laugh. Think about how often you laugh. To help with your thinking, answer the following questions about what makes you laugh. To finish, work on your own or with others to write a funny story that makes you laugh and you think will make others laugh. If you require extra room to write, use the back of this page.

What makes you laugh and why?

....

....

How long ago did you last have a big laugh?

....

....

What happened that make you laugh so much?

....

....

How did laughing like that make you feel?

....

....

Write a funny story that will make you and others laugh.

....

....

....

....

9.4 Balanced Breath – teacher notes

ACTIVITY OBJECTIVES

- Children begin to see the connection between breathing calmly and reducing stress in their body.

- Children are introduced to different types of breathing techniques.

- Children develop some familiarity with different breathing techniques.

WORKSHEET REQUIREMENTS

You will need:

Breathe calmly

- A4 paper

MAIN ACTIVITY

- Children use the worksheet as an introduction to practising breathing techniques.

- Helper schedules a time and follows through with different breathing techniques for different times in the day and over the week. Helper asks the children to keep a daily journal of their breathing exercises.

- Children learn about the heart rate–breathing–calming connection. With a partner, children record their heart rate before and after the breathing exercise.

EXTENSION ACTIVITIES

- Children lead peers/family members through the range of breathing exercises.

- Children ask peers/staff/family members for more breathing exercise ideas. They then present their ideas to their group.

- Children, working in small groups, design a breathing ideas sequence storybook for use in their class/family.

9.4 Balanced Breath

Controlling your breathing is a good way to help you relax your body, particularly when your body is tense and you are worrying or becoming overly excited. Calm, slow breathing can assist you in calming your body and your mind.

Breathe calmly

Below we have provided you with five different types of controlled breathing.

Practise these with your helper/peers.

1. Counting breathing

Using your regular breathing… Breathe in counting 1, 2, 3 then breathe out counting 4, 5, 6.

2. 'I am' breathing

Using regular breathing… Breathe in thinking 'I am relaxed' then breathe out thinking 'I am calm.'

3. Colour breathing

Using regular breathing… Breathe in and think of the colour red, breathe out thinking of the colour orange, etc., until you have completed all the colours of the rainbow.

4. Belly breathing

Using regular breathing… Breathe in and imagine that you are breathing air into your belly button, breathe out and imagine that you are expelling air out of your belly button.

5. Muscle breathing

Using regular breathing… Breathe in and clench your fists, breathe out, relax your fists. Breathe in and squeeze your eyes shut, breathe out and relax your eyes. Continue doing the same with other muscles in your body, such as those in your legs, arms, neck, etc.

9.5 Kitchen Kicks – teacher notes

ACTIVITY OBJECTIVES

- Children learn more about the role of exercise in reducing stress levels.

- Children begin to see the connection between stress, exercise and relaxation.

- Children develop their enthusiasm for exercise as a mind and body stress reducer.

WORKSHEET REQUIREMENTS

You will need:

- Wooden spoon

- Weights e.g. packet of pasta

- Bowl, eggs and whisk

- Chair

- Cookbooks

- Step ladder

MAIN ACTIVITY

- Children perform at least one of the exercises on the worksheet on a daily basis – before breakfast at home and before first break at school.

- Children do their exercises both slowly and quickly and discuss which speed worked best for them in terms of energising and then relaxing.

- Children teach their exercises to younger children/family members.

- Children develop an exercise schedule and stick with it.

EXTENSION ACTIVITIES

- Children perform the exercise as an aerobic 'follow the leader' exercise game.

- Children record their personal best for each exercise over a fortnightly period.

- Children cut off the fingers from a pair of old fabric gloves. They decorate each finger as an imaginary peer or family member. They take their finger puppet on the exercise regime.

9.5 Kitchen Kicks

Exercise is great for relaxing and for energising. It helps you deal with tension, keeps you energetic and helps your body relax afterwards.

We have provided you with some fun exercise suggestions – they are unique exercises keeping with the theme of cooking.

Together with your helper choose which ones you want to try, a few or all of them. Make sure you are in a safe place for your exercises – remember that although you are using kitchen equipment, it may be dangerous to perform exercises in the kitchen. Ask your helper for advice about safe places to exercise and then decide on your safe location.

Have fun, as you get active!

- karate kicks

- wooden spoon star jumps (hold a wooden spoon in each hand while performing star jumps)

- weight exercises holding a packet of pasta or plastic water bottle

- jogging around kitchen bench or table

- use your arms to beat a bowl of eggs

- yoga stretches using a chair

- hop over a cookbook

- balance yourself on one leg holding a table/bench

- pretend you are stacking the dishwasher by squatting

- use your muscles and help carry the groceries

- use rowing movements and 'sweep' the floor

- step on and off the step ladder.

9.6 Sleep Strategies – teacher notes

ACTIVITY OBJECTIVES

- Children expand their knowledge about the importance of relaxing activities as opposed to energising activities at the end of the day.

- Children are introduced to a variety of relaxing activities appropriate for downtime at the end of the day.

- Children take more ownership of what relaxing activities they will include in their bedtime routine.

WORKSHEET REQUIREMENTS

You will need:

- Coloured A4 paper or card

- Pen/pencil

MAIN ACTIVITY

- Children begin thinking about what does and doesn't aid sleep by completing the worksheet activity. They can then mind map other helpful and unhelpful ways of winding their bodies and minds down at the end of the day so going to sleep happens easily. They separate the ideas into the two columns on the worksheet – Relaxing and Energising. Children nominate which column of ideas their own night time behaviours belong with. They tally their responses and discuss the findings.

- Children interview older people about what they did when they were young when it was time for bed. Children record their responses and share them with the group.

- Children write a letter to their parent/s naming the relaxing activities they would like to include in their home bedtime routine. They role-play these choices before going home so that they can model them for their parent/s.

EXTENSION ACTIVITIES

- Children compile a 'Smart things to do at bedtime' reference book.

- Children silkscreen a picture of someone important/something of importance (e.g. family photo, Transformer, ballet shoes, etc.) onto their pillowcase.

- Children create a night sky mobile that may or may not glow in the dark. The mobile comes out when it is time for sleep.

9.6 Sleep Strategies

Sometimes you just can't get to sleep, and it doesn't matter what you or your parent/carer do or suggest, nothing seems to works!

The trick is to work out what relaxes and what energises you. We know that we need to be relaxed to get to sleep. If we are too energised then we may find it hard to fall asleep.

Below is a list of a mix of relaxing and energising activities. Sort out whether they are relaxing or energising, write them down in the chart, and then discuss your choices with your helper/class. Write a plan for yourself when you have trouble falling asleep. You might like to have this plan in your room for reference.

When I can't sleep I:

- play quietly with my…

- read a book for… minutes

- listen to calming music for… minutes

- have a night light on

- listen to rock music

- run around the house

- call out across the house

- listen to a visualisation

- use some breathing techniques

- write my worries down

- eat food

- throw a tantrum.

✓

Relaxing	Energising

My plan for when I am having trouble sleeping is to

....

....

....

....

....

....

....

....

....

10 Rights and Responsibilities – History Themed

Importance of the capability

Rights are guaranteed conditions. They are what you should always expect. Responsibilities are something you are always expected to do. They are a way you are expected to behave. Enjoying a right requires everyone to accept certain responsibilities. For example: 'To protect our right to be safe, we will use materials appropriately and walk (not run) in class.'

Children who have learned to be responsible are trustworthy individuals. They do not blame others for their mistakes or misfortunes. They can be trusted and depended on to do things on their own. They make responsible choices to stay out of trouble.

By using 'I' messages instead of 'You' messages children learn to take more responsibility for their needs and to express them in a more assertive manner.

List of activities

10.1 Rights and Responsibilities   –   Rights and responsibilities table

10.2 Creative Captain   –   Creative writing

10.3 Daily Duties   –   Responsibilities chart

10.4 Rules Rule   –   Connecting chart

10.5 Connection Chart   –   Rights and responsibilities flow chart

10.6 Knight Right   –   Rights and responsibilities stories

10.1 Rights and Responsibilities – teacher notes

ACTIVITY OBJECTIVES

- Children learn to differentiate between responsibilities (something you are always expected to do) and rights (guaranteed conditions – something you should always expect).

- Children begin to understand that enjoying a right requires everyone to accept certain responsibilities.

- Children reflect on their rights and responsibilities as a class member and family member.

WORKSHEET REQUIREMENTS

You will need:

- A4 coloured paper

- Scissors

- Pen/pencil

MAIN ACTIVITY

- Children distinguish between a right and a responsibility at home and at school.

- Children talk about the differences between rights and responsibilities, and explore why a right in one situation might sometimes become a responsibility in another situation.

- Children use the worksheet to begin connecting rights to their corresponding responsibilities, and vice versa.

EXTENSION ACTIVITIES

- Children make a rights and responsibilities interconnecting jigsaw by discussing their rights and responsibilities, recording them in a table, laminating the table and then cutting it into pieces. The jigsaw can have as many pieces as you like.

- Children make a scrapbook about rights and responsibilities; they could include photographs, drawings or collages of people that demonstrate their rights and responsibilities (e.g. moving around carefully), or cut pictures from magazines, categorise them as rights or responsibilities, and say what right or responsibility they depict.

- Children mind map rights and responsibilities in the school, family and community.

- Children draw some of their rights and associated responsibilities.

- Children research rights and accompanying responsibilities for children in other parts of the world.

- Children write a newspaper advertisement promoting a children's theme park. The most important information for this advertisement is the rights and responsibilities that are in place to ensure everyone has fun.

- Children produce a PowerPoint about a classroom with lots of rights but no responsibilities.

10.1 Rights and Responsibilities

Let's have a look at what a right is and what a responsibility is.

A right is something that you should always expect to have.

A responsibility is something that you should always do and is expected of you.

For example, you have the right to be respected, so you have the responsibility to respect yourself and others.

We have made up a rights and responsibilities table for you – some is filled in, some is incomplete. Your task is to:

- complete the table

- discuss and compare with your helper/peers and see if you can come up with other examples

- display your rights and responsibilities table in your class.

Rights	Responsibilities
I have the right to be myself	My responsibility is to be myself
I have the right to be respected	My responsibility is to respect others and myself
I have the right to be peaceful	
	My responsibility is not to destroy the property of others
I have the right to hear and to be heard	
	My responsibility is to keep myself safe

10.2 Creative Captain – teacher notes

ACTIVITY OBJECTIVES

- Children classify rights and responsibilities with rules.

- Children begin to see the connection between rights, responsibilities and rules – rules let everyone know their responsibilities and safeguard the rights of everyone.

- Children use the medium of storytelling to explain what might happen when rights, responsibilities and rules are aligned.

WORKSHEET REQUIREMENTS

You will need:

- A4 paper

- Pen/pencil

MAIN ACTIVITY

- Children use the worksheet as a creative introduction to ideas about rights, responsibilities and rules. They use discussion and creative writing to develop their ideas.

- Working in small groups, children dramatise rights and responsibilities of being aboard their ship.

- Children sequence rights, responsibilities and rules – in the imaginary world of the ship's captain and the real world of the classroom/family.

EXTENSION ACTIVITIES

- Children mind map the differences between a right and a responsibility.

- Children design a bookmark with rights on one side and responsibilities on the other side.

- Children examine their class and family rules to see the rights and responsibilities underpinning them.

- Children think about rights and responsibilities for different years/class groups in their school. They note similarities and differences.

- Children ask their parents questions about rights and responsibilities in their work life.

10.2 Creative Captain

Captains are responsible people whom we trust to keep us safe when we travel with them. They make sure that having a right requires everyone to accept and perform certain responsibilities. They have rules to let everyone know what these responsibilities are. In this way they make sure everyone's rights are safeguarded.

On the next page we have provided you with a fictional scenario where you may face some rights and responsibilities challenges.

- Read the introduction to the story.
- Think about, chat about and write answers for the Rights and Responsibilities questions below.
- Share your answers with your helper/peers.
- Finish off your story with some creative writing.

What are your daily responsibilities?

....

....

....

....

What are your new responsibilities after the Captain has made his announcement?

....

....

....

....

What are your rights?

....

....

....

....

Introduction

You are a cabin boy/girl working on a ship. Every day you swab the deck, knot the ropes and help the cook. The Captain has ordered all crew on deck for an important announcement. He has detected a pirate ship nearby.

The Captain's responsibility is to keep his crew and ship safe from harm and he needs help from all his crew. Therefore the ship must prepare for battle in case it is an unfriendly pirate ship.

....

....

....

....

....

....

....

....

....

....

....

....

....

....

....

....

....

....

....

....

10.3 Daily Duties – teacher notes

ACTIVITY OBJECTIVES

- Children deepen their understanding of the relationship between school rules, rights and expected responsibilities.

- Children identify rights and responsibilities underlying their school/class/ family rules.

- Children think about what they do that demonstrates responsibility.

WORKSHEET REQUIREMENTS

You will need:

- A4 coloured paper

- Pen/pencil

MAIN ACTIVITY

- Children discuss 'what is responsibility?'

- Children give examples of occasions when they have behaved in a responsible way.

- Children link their responsibilities with rights.

- Children transfer this information into a weekly responsibility chart on the worksheet.

- Children discuss situations in which they behaved in a responsible manner.

- Children predict what rights are connected with their responsible behaviours.

EXTENSION ACTIVITIES

- In small groups, children compile a class responsibilities chart for creating a garden.

- Children take photographs of their classmates and family members behaving in a responsible manner, either in their normal activities or through role-play.

- Children create a code with the words 'rights, responsibilities, rules'.

10.3 Daily Duties

I'm doing my job

Have you chosen to take on chores/duties at home, school or within your community? Are you trusted to carry out your duties in a responsible manner every day? What are the rights you are protecting when you do your duties responsibly?

Below we have provided you with a Daily Duties table where you can make notes about your responsibilities.

You can enlarge this to poster size as a reminder tool.

	Home	**School**	**Community**
Example	*Feed the cat*	*Listen to teacher*	*Throw litter in bin*
Monday			
Tuesday			
Wednesday			
Thursday			
Friday			
Saturday			
Sunday			
Every day			

10.4 Rules Rule – teacher notes

ACTIVITY OBJECTIVES

- Children deepen their understanding of the connection between baseline school rules, underlying rights and expected responsibilities.

- Children understand that rights and responsibilities are the foundation of/ springboard for baseline school rules.

- Children identify the rights and responsibilities underlying their baseline school/class rules.

WORKSHEET REQUIREMENTS

You will need:

- A4 or A3 card (enlarge if required)

- Velcro dots

- Laminating device

- Non-permanent marker

MAIN ACTIVITY

- Children discuss rules, responsibilities and rights then use their conclusions to complete the worksheet activity.

- Children write a letter to a new student advising on the rights and responsibilities underpinning their class/school rules.

- Children teach a classmate their class rules, emphasising the rights and responsibilities for each rule.

- Children develop a class covenant based on their rights, responsibilities and class rules.

EXTENSION ACTIVITIES

- Children distinguish between the rights and responsibilities underlying family rules and class rules.

- Children compose a song about the rights and responsibilities underlying societal rules.

- Children debate what changes they would like to make to existing class/ school rules, making sure that rights and responsibilities are upheld.

10.4 Rules Rule

Using your school/class rules, connect each rule with the right that goes with it, and the responsibility that also goes with it.

We have provided you with two examples. Laminate this page, then write in your own responses using a non-permanent marker. You may like to display your Rules–Rights–Responsibilities poster in your classroom.

Rules	Rights	Responsibilities
Speak courteously	To be spoken to kindly	To use kind words
Be safe, stay safe	To be safe	To stay safe

10.5 Connection Chart – teacher notes

ACTIVITY OBJECTIVES

- Children deepen their understanding of what a right is.

- Children broaden their comprehension of what a responsibility is.

- Children begin to see the connection between an event, its underlying right and associated responsibility, resulting in a consequence.

WORKSHEET REQUIREMENTS

You will need:

- A4 paper

- Pen/pencil

MAIN ACTIVITY

- Children use the worksheet activity to consider the accompanying responsibilities, rights and consequences for an event.

- Children make a flow chart sequencing events, rules, rights and responsibilities and consequences.

- Children make a booklet about the rights and responsibilities and accompanying consequences for their class rules.

- Children paint a mural illustrating the rights, responsibilities and consequence sequence. They talk about what happens when people do not accept their responsibilities.

EXTENSION ACTIVITIES

- Children make a cartoon strip showing what consequences occur when people follow and do not follow the sequence between rights and responsibilities.

10.5 Connection Chart

With rights come responsibilities.

Discuss the events below in the Connection Chart with your helper/class and make connections between the right, the responsibility and the consquence related to the event.

Be safe

Event	Right	Responsibility	Consequence
Scribbled on school desk	For my desk to be clean and safe	Not to graffiti mine/other's desk	Clean the desk
Mucking around in class	To learn at school without distractions	Listen, think and learn at school without interrupting	See class rules
Ignoring chores at home			
Forgetting to bring lunch to school			
Teasing or being unkind to others			

10.6 Knight Right – teacher notes

ACTIVITY OBJECTIVES

- Children deepen their understanding of rights and responsibilities.
- Children connect rights with responsibilities.
- Children think about their own rights and accompanying responsibilities.

WORKSHEET REQUIREMENTS

You will need:

- A4 paper
- Pen/pencil
- Scissors

MAIN ACTIVITY

- Children distinguish between rights and responsibilities using the worksheet activity.
- Children decorate their rights and responsibilities shields.
- Children compare and contrast their rights and responsibilities shields.

EXTENSION ACTIVITIES

- Children play charades, acting out the 'right', and the audience name the accompanying 'responsibility'.
- Children make up a poem about their rights and responsibilities.
- Children make up a chart of what happens when people accept their rights but do not accept their responsibilities.

10.6 Knights Right

Inside the shields, draw or write some of the rights you think you have, and then inside the banner draw or write the responsibility that goes with each right.

Decorate your shields and compare them with your friends' shields.

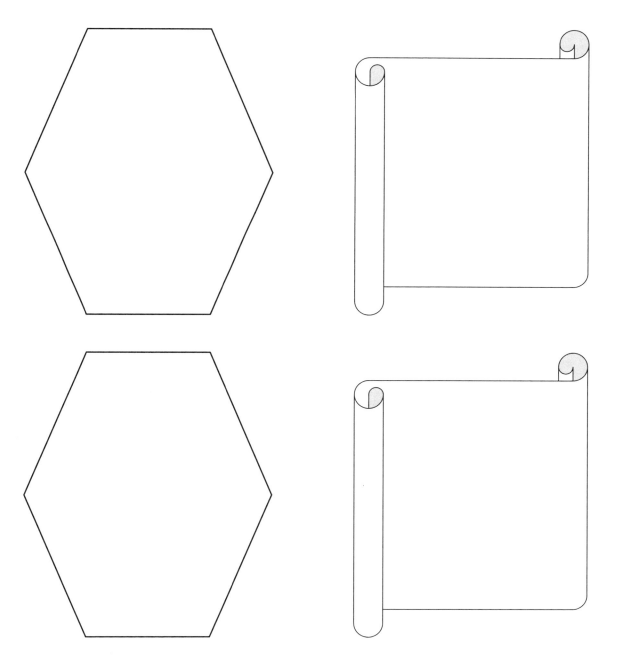

Conclusion

One of the major challenges of childhood is developing social competence, self-confidence and a willingness to want to achieve to the best of one's ability. As children grow and develop, they are refining and mastering their social cognition in domains including organisation, persistence, confidence, sociability, emotion regulation, independence, effective communication, relaxation and rights and responsibilities. While gaining proficiency in these domains is the work of a lifetime, it begins in childhood.

Children develop at varying rates and in different ways in these social developmental domains. When we want to encourage children to develop their social cognition we need to build on knowledge that they already have. As explained in Vygotsky's sociocultural theory (Daniels 1996; Vygotsky 1978), many developmental tasks occur in the *zone of proximal development*. This zone refers to the range of tasks that a child cannot yet accomplish without assistance from peers and/or adults with greater knowledge, but is just about ready to accomplish once given the necessary support. The framework of this support is called 'scaffolding'.

Children's social competence development is scaffolded when they have opportunities to practise and refine newly acquired skills with support from peers and/or adults. Throughout this process, children are challenged just beyond the level of their present mastery.

Children construct their social knowledge through increasingly complex contexts that involve real-life experiences and play that they have initiated themselves or within adult-initiated and/or planned experiences. These experiences give them developmentally appropriate and culturally relevant opportunities to develop more intricate thinking, social exposure and emotional security.

Children are active agents involved in their own learning. This learning involves the process of making sense of information and of comprehending and mastering skills and knowledge as a result of interacting within a supportive learning environment.

With this in mind, the following guidelines for teaching children social thinking and emotional well-being have been the building blocks on which *Social Success* is based.

A social thinking curriculum:

- builds on what children already know and are able to do

- consolidates learning and promotes acquisition of new knowledge, skills, processes and concepts

- promotes the development of knowledge, comprehension, processes and skills

- is integrated across a range of disciplines

- is learner-centred, adult-supported and outcomes-oriented

- has meaningful and pertinent content

- is user-friendly and achievable for all children

- supports and extends children's development and learning

- has goals that are credible, relevant and attainable

- is responsive to each child's diverse and unique social, emotional, developmental and learning needs and circumstances.

Our greatest gift to children is a strong grounding in social thinking, emotional well-being and social competence.

References

Anderson, J.R. (1982) 'Acquisition of cognitive skills.' *Psychological Review 89*, 369–406.

Australian Scholarships Group (ASG) (2007) *Student Social and Emotional Health Report.* Oakleigh, Victoria. Available at www.asg.com.au/Page.aspx?ID=436, accessed on 14 December 2010.

Bandura, A. (1997) *Self-efficacy: The Exercise of Control.* New York: Freeman.

Bellini, S. (2006) *Building Social Relationships: A Systematic Approach to Teaching Social Interaction Skills to Children and Adolescents with Autism Spectrum Disorders and Other Social Difficulties.* Shawnee Mission, KS: Autism Asperger Publishing Company.

Bernard, M. (2004) *The You Can Do It! Education Early Childhood Program.* Melbourne: The Australian Scholarship Group.

Caprara, G.V., Barbaranelli, C., Pastorelli, C., Bandura, A. and Zimbardo, P.G. (2000) 'Prosocial foundations of children's academic achievement.' *Psychological Science 11*, 302–6.

Carter, M.A. (2009) *Take a Stand, Lend a Hand … Stop Bullying Now.* Queensland, Australia: M.A. Carter Consultancy.

Covington, M. (1992) *Making the Grade: A Self-worth Perspective on Motivation and School Reform.* New York: Cambridge University Press.

Damon, W. (1999) 'The moral development of children.' *Scientific American 281*, 2, 72–88.

Daniels, H. (ed.) (1996) *An Introduction to Vygotsky.* London: Routledge.

Gardner, H. (1983) *Frames of Mind: The Theory of Multiple Intelligences.* New York: Basic Books.

Gardner, H. (1993) *Multiple Intelligences: The Theory in Practice.* New York: Basic Books.

Martin, A. (2003) *How to Motivate Your Child.* Sydney: Bantam Books.

Martin, A. (2005) *How to Help Your Child Fly through Life.* Sydney: Bantam Books.

Nicholls, J.G. (1989) *The Competitive Ethos and Democratic Education.* Cambridge, MA: Harvard University Press.

Skiffington, S. and Zeus, P. (2003) *Behavioral Coaching: Building Sustainable Personal and Organizational Strengths.* Sydney: McGraw-Hill.

Vygotsky, L.S. (1978). *Mind and Society: The Development of Higher Psychological Processes.* Cambridge, MA: Harvard University Press.

Solutions

Solution to Empty Emotions Anagrams, Activity 6.3

Top row: MAD, SCARED, BRAVE, CALM

Bottom row: SAD, HAPPY, WORRIED, PROUD

Solution to Word Puzzle Crack the Code, Activity 7.6

```
E  D  U  T  I  T  T  A  +  +  +  E  C  S  +
M  Y  S  E  L  F  +  +  +  +  +  C  +  O  S  +
+  +  +  +  +  +  +  +  +  N  +  +  N  E  +
+  +  +  +  +  +  +  +  E  +  +  +  F  C  +
+  +  +  +  +  +  +  D  +  +  +  +  I  C  +
D  R  E  S  P  O  N  S  I  B  L  E  D  U  +
+  E  +  +  +  E  +  E  C  +  L  +  E  S  +
+  +  T  +  P  +  C  H  F  B  +  +  N  +  +
+  +  +  E  +  +  A  I  A  F  +  +  C  +  +
+  +  D  +  R  L  +  P  T  +  O  +  E  +  +
+  N  +  +  L  M  A  +  +  C  +  R  +  +  +
I  +  +  E  +  C  I  +  +  +  A  +  T  +  +
+  +  N  +  +  +  +  N  +  +  +  R  +  +  +
+  G  +  +  +  +  +  +  E  +  +  +  P  +  +
E  +  +  +  +  +  +  +  +  D  +  +  +  +  +
```

(Across, Down, Direction)

ATTITUDE (8,1,W)

CAPABLE (6,12,NE)

CHALLENGE (9,7,SW)

CONFIDENCE (13,1,S)

DETERMINED (1,6,SE)

EFFORT (8,7,SE)

INDEPENDENCE (1,12,NE)

MYSELF (1,2,E)

PRACTICE (13,14,NW)

RESPONSIBLE (2,6,E)

SUCCESS (14,7,N)

Solution to Jargon Jumble, Activity 8.6

JOINING IN

WAIT FOR THE RIGHT TIME

SAY, 'CAN I JOIN IN' OR 'CAN I PLAY TOO'

TAKE A BIG BREATH BEFORE ASKING TO JOIN IN

STOP, LOOK AROUND AND THINK IF THIS IS THE RIGHT TIME TO JOIN IN

LISTENING

REPLY, GET MORE INFORMATION OR DO AS ASKED

THINK ABOUT WHAT IS BEING SAID

STAY STILL, QUIET AND CALM

STOP, THINK AND LOOK IN THE DIRECTION OF THE SPEAKER

WAITING YOUR TURN

TAKE SOME DEEP BREATHS AND WAIT QUIETLY

WAIT FOR THE RIGHT TIME AND HAVE YOUR TURN

STOP AND THINK 'IT'S HARD TO WAIT, BUT I CAN DO IT'

COOPERATING

SHARE YOUR IDEAS

LISTEN TO OTHERS' IDEAS

GET MORE INFORMATION IF NECESSARY

STOP, THINK AND LISTEN TO THE DIRECTIONS